"We are save _____ ____ Christ but into the _____ _____ or his church. In an age of extreme individualism and profound loneliness, Barnabas gives us a glimpse into the church's purpose and beauty, her shared values and challenges, inviting us to take our place in something greater than ourselves: the communion of saints. Here is good help for all who long to belong."

JEN WILKIN, Bible Teacher; Author, *None Like Him*

"Our local churches, despite their flaws and imperfections, are purposed by Jesus to be a taste of heaven on earth. With pastoral warmth and biblical wisdom, Barnabas paints a picture in these pages of what our experience in the church is meant to be. This book is deeply refreshing and grounded with helpful application."

ADAM RAMSEY, Lead Pastor, Liberti Church, Gold Coast, Australia; Network Director, Acts 29 Asia Pacific

"In our time, when loneliness is at epidemic proportions, something proactive must be done. As Barnabas shows, the local church is the epicenter for belonging to be experienced in the richest, most life-giving and sustainable ways. I cannot recommend this book to you highly enough."

SCOTT SAULS, Senior Pastor, Christ Presbyterian Church, Nashville; Author, *A Gentle Answer*

"Most Christians really want to connect with and to serve their local congregations. They often just don't know how or where to start. Barnabas Piper does away with hectoring or manipulation and offers accessible and wise counsel on how to find that kind of love and belonging within the community of Christ."

RUSSELL MOORE, Editor-in-Chief, *Christianity Today*

"In an age of isolation, individualism, and loneliness, the church has a wonderful opportunity to remind people that they were made for community—made to belong to the family of God, the church. *Belong* is a book that can help Christians retrieve the priority of the local church. I am praying this book gets a wide reading."

J.T. ENGLISH, Lead Pastor, Storyline Church, Arvada, Colorado; Author, *Deep Discipleship*

"Jesus is inviting us to truly belong to a church community full of humility, honesty, and honour. Part of the value of this book is that its author has experienced the pain of churches where belonging was hard and the attempt to belong left him weary and wary. Whether you are loving church life, scared of stepping through the doors of another church, or somewhere in between, this book will be valuable to you."

JOHN HINDLEY, Pastor, BroadGrace, Norfolk, UK;
Author, *Serving without Sinking* and *Refreshed*

"Barnabas Piper helpfully reminds us about what it really means to belong to a church family in a way that is full of heart and life. I highly recommend this book—it will challenge and inspire you to think differently about your church and love your church family more deeply and authentically."

JENNY REES, Chair, Southern Women's Convention, UK

"This book is a welcome and needed vision for creating church cultures that warmly reflect the gospel. It is an encouragement for each of us to be the church we hope to be a part of—loving one another, encouraging one another, bearing with one another, and serving one another."

MELISSA KRUGER, Director of Women's Initiatives for
The Gospel Coalition; Author, *Growing Together*

"The church of Jesus Christ is designed by God to be a celebration of the miracle of belonging. Because of the grace of Jesus, we belong to God and to one another. In a way that I have never read before, Barnabas Piper not only defines that belonging but also helps us to understand how to live with one another in a way that always reflects that, by grace, we together belong to God."

PAUL TRIPP, Author, *New Morning Mercies*

"For too long, we have viewed church (whether consciously or not) as consumers. Barnabas provides a much-needed corrective to help us see and value what it means to belong. Here is wise counsel and radical yet biblical therapy for us all."

ADRIAN REYNOLDS, Head of National Ministries, FIEC, UK

belong

BARNABAS PIPER

Belong
Loving Your Church by Reflecting Christ to One Another
© 2023 Barnabas Piper

Published by:
The Good Book Company

thegoodbook.com | thegoodbook.co.uk
thegoodbook.com.au | thegoodbook.co.nz | thegoodbook.co.in

Cover design by Faceout Studio | Art direction and design by André Parker

ISBN: 9781784988227 | Printed in the UK

This book is dedicated to my dear friends from my community group at Immanuel Nashville.

You have shown me what belonging to the family of God looks like and invited me into it through your honesty, compassion, hospitality, humility, humor, constancy, and faithfulness to Jesus through so many joys and sorrows. Together we have experienced the profoundly normal and supernatural reality of fellowship in Jesus. I love you all.

Thank you.

CONTENTS

FOREWORD

BY RAY ORTLUND

You belong to Christ.
Mark 9:41

God created us to belong, both to him and to one another. But our pride drove us far away, both from him and from one another. Now Jesus is bringing us back, both to him and to one another.

Belonging is an adjustment for every one of us. Maybe there was a time when we felt so superior that belonging was beneath us. Or maybe we felt safer in our own guarded aloofness. Or maybe we feared that belonging might pull us into commitments we couldn't live up to. But if you have picked up this book, you are at least open to belonging. This book will help you to see your options more clearly and to make your decisions more confidently.

Here's why your future will get better by bravely jumping in. Jesus is not out to save isolated individuals scattered here and there. He is creating and gathering a new community in which everyone deeply belongs, both to him and to one another. And when we finally belong— really belong—to a group of people whom we respect and enjoy, it feels *so good*. We've come home.

I admit, it isn't easy to get there. It can be even harder to stay there. If the belonging we all desire were simple and formulaic, the experience would be common. In fact, for me, it can be difficult to stop and think about belonging. The topic stirs painful memories. I know what it's like to discover that I did *not* belong. I thought I did, but I was wrong. And it hurt. Maybe that's been your experience too. Churches can make belonging hard and even risky— which is to say, churches can make it hard to experience Jesus. And that is not ok.

Barnabas Piper has written this wonderful book because he understands from personal experience both how hard and how glorious belonging can be. He is qualified to help the rest of us think it through. I believe you will find in Barnabas a trustworthy guide, because his experience is deep and his conclusions are honest. Most importantly, Barnabas is a faithful follower of Jesus. The Lord gently led him from the outer margins all the way to the deepest heart of Immanuel Church in Nashville. I watched Barnabas walk that journey. Sometimes it was painful. Other times it was joyful. Always it was Jesus leading Barnabas closer to his heart. From his early cautious explorations all the way to his eventual glad commitments, Barnabas kept on saying yes to Jesus. And now he is helping us make Immanuel a safe place for still others to belong. His story looks to me like the newness of life that Jesus died and rose again to create.

Barnabas wisely counsels us, "The church is the only place where we can heal from the hurt we've encountered in church." If he's right—and he is—then this book might open a door for you to heal in surprising ways.

So, I commend to you this book by my friend Barnabas. He is a man who can truly say, "Follow my example, as I follow the example of Christ" (1 Corinthians 11:1, CSB).

Ray Ortlund
Renewal Ministries
August 2022

INTRODUCTION

WHO THIS BOOK IS FOR

In the summer of 2017 I walked through the doors of Immanuel Church in Nashville for the first time. I was a few months removed from a painful divorce and a few months into searching for a new church home. Both experiences had left me spiritually exhausted and emotionally discouraged, uncertain of my future, and uncomfortable in church.

I grew up in the church—quite literally, as I'm a pastor's kid. I had been part of churches for my entire life, sometimes feeling joyfully at home, sometimes feeling like I was in the middle of a family feud on steroids, and other times feeling like the outsider. I was intimately familiar with the best and worst the church had to offer, and I knew I needed to be part of one.

But I wasn't at all sure I *wanted* to be.

I sat in the furthest back corner of the service that day and did my best to meet nobody (my usual strategy when visiting churches). When the service began, a pastor stood up and welcomed the congregation warmly. *Probably phony*, I thought. Then he proceeded to say these words:

> *To all who are weary and need rest;*
> *To all who mourn and long for comfort;*
> *To all who fail and need strength;*
> *To all who sin and need a Savior;*
> *This church opens wide her doors and her heart with a*
> *welcome from Jesus Christ.*

Beautiful words, comforting words, welcoming words; words I desperately wanted to believe—but words I instinctively rejected. I didn't think the pastor was lying, per se. I just thought it was aspirational nonsense. In my experience churches usually declare what they want to be, not what they are. They advertise their mission and vision, but are less clear on their present state. *If only a church actually welcomed people like that, I might find a home*, I thought. I had enough self-awareness to know that I was particularly cynical about churches, so rather than walk away with an eye roll and a snarky tweet, I decided to let the church prove itself to me either as a place of welcome or as a place of hypocrisy.

What I found in the two years following that first cynical Sunday was a place of belonging. It was a place of safety for the weary and broken. Honesty was upheld as a value: speaking the truth about our lives and our spiritual state and our needs. People were treated with the God-given dignity they deserved, even as they were honest about the ugliness in their lives. And it all worked because it was done in humility before God and in dependence on Jesus.

The pastors and leaders exemplified this, but it was the members who embodied honesty, safety, honor, and humility week in and week out to me, so that God could work in my life. It was in conversations over drinks, in living rooms on Sunday afternoons, and in weeknight Bible study and prayer with other men that my heart was thawed and my eyes were opened to what church could be. I had found a church home, a place of belonging to the family of God. Out of this belonging God healed and restored me, gave me strength, tempered my cynicism, and eventually called me to full-time pastoral ministry.

So it is, that in what to me is the unlikeliest turn of events, I have the privilege of serving as a pastor at Immanuel now. When I stand in front of the congregation on Sunday mornings and welcome people, I think of where I was in 2017. Each time I open my mouth to say those words, "To all who are weary and need rest...", I pray that the people in that room will find *belonging* in that welcome from Jesus.

That's who this book is for—the person figuring out what it means to belong to a church and whether it is worth it. You may love the church and desire to commit more deeply and serve better. You may be skeptical and reluctant because of past experiences, but you believe

God wants you in his church. You may be wounded and cautious, fearful even, because of damage inflicted on you through the church. You may be a brand-new believer, unsure what to think about church. Or you may be uprooted, having relocated from a place of familiarity to be dropped in a new town and new church where you hope to find a home.

My hope is that this book shows what it looks like to belong in church, really and truly, and what it looks like to help others to do the same.

1. WHAT DOES IT MEAN TO BELONG?

Let me set your mind at ease about this book, or maybe disabuse you of false notions. I neither want you to be intimidated by what you think is in these pages, nor do I want you to be disappointed by what you don't find.

In these pages you will not find a list of qualifications for church membership against which you can measure yourself. Nor will you find an explanation or defense of church membership as a system or structure. My aim is not to give a survey of how membership works in different denominations or traditions. I am writing about *belonging*, and while there is a close connection with formal membership, they are not the same. A person can be a member of a church without belonging, and a person can belong to a church that does not offer formal membership. The pressing question is not about processes or polity but about connection to and closeness within the body of Christ.

This is not a book primarily for pastors or church leaders either, except inasmuch as they are members of the body too. I'm not here to write about marks, measurements, or metrics of a healthy church. Nor will you find a manual on how to recruit or assimilate people into church membership. Rather, my hope is that any church leaders who read this will see themselves as one of the sheep, under Christ our Shepherd, part of this family of God.

Finally, I will not lance a boil of church bitterness in these pages. I have experience of being hurt by churchgoers and church leaders alike. You very well might too. Disillusionment with church comes easily. I've found that dwelling on it doesn't help me love Jesus or his church more. And make no mistake, it is *his* church.

I played football in high school, and the coaches would sometimes have us watch our own game film so we could review our performances and correct errors. Our team was exceptionally bad, so those film sessions were mostly an exercise in the coaches disgustedly yelling, "Look how much y'all suck; be better!" (Poor coaching may have contributed to our overall lack of success.) That's not my aim in this book, either. Yes, the church has some "bad film," with plenty of lowlights, and we can be better. But how to be better, rather than what sucks, is what I will focus on in these chapters.

AN INVITATION

When I say the church can be "better" I am not merely judging by my experiences or preferences. I am looking at it through the descriptions and prescriptions of the Bible. It doesn't much matter what you or I want the church to be like if that differs from what God wants his church to be like. So that needs to be our standard, and then we need to consider how we fit into God's design for the church.

This book is, more than anything else, an invitation. I'm inviting you to see the church, in its local expressions, as God sees it. It's an invitation to see his plan and his heart's desire for it, and to step into your place in that plan. The Bible offers a transcendent, beautiful, transformative portrait of the church, and we were designed by our Creator to be part of it.

You may have heard preachers refer to the church as "God's design" or "God's strategy" or something similar. While those descriptions are entirely true, they can feel mechanized and impersonal. Most of us don't show up to church with a yearning to be part of a plan. We don't go through the pains of searching for a new church in a new city after moving across the country because we want to fit into a grand strategy. We are looking for something personal, something deeply meaningful, something with which we can identify. God wants you to find that in a local church—so this book is an invitation to do just that. Yes, God's plan for his church is strategic—but part of his perfect strategy is offering hurting, tired, worn-out, needy sinners like you and me a place to belong. His plan for his church is that it be a place to encounter the profound, transformative, healing, restoring grace of Jesus Christ, together.

That is what I am inviting you into. Or rather, this is what the Bible invites you into, and I am doing my best to pass it along with clarity, hope, and beauty.

FINDING THAT FEELING

Pretty much everybody yearns to belong somewhere or to something, and life is a constant sliding scale of feeling a greater or lesser sense of belonging in whatever context. It's easy to recognize the power of belonging in social subcultures. In the 1960s people came together as hippies, a counter-culture for those who were pushing back against corporate and governmental sensibilities and expectations. In the 1990s something similar happened in the punk-rock scene as young people lashed out at "sell-out" pop culture. Today there is a massive subculture of gamers, complete with its own celebrities and vernacular. In each instance people who didn't feel as if they fit in mainstream society found something to be part of, a place to fit, a place of belonging.

We see the same draw in more mainstream parts of culture as well. I live in Tennessee, smack in the heart of the college football cult land (um, I mean, the middle of college football's most dedicated fandom): the Southeastern United States. There is a whole culture of fandom—team colors, team slogans, tailgate parties, flags on trucks and houses (and on trucks as big as houses), trash talk, emotional roller-coasters, superiority (Alabama), inferiority (Auburn), detachment (Kentucky), and denial (Tennessee). If you are *in* it, you have a sense of belonging. If you, like me, don't care all that much about college football, that last sentence made you feel left on the outside, and if you live in this area of the US, you can sense you are something of an outsider on autumn Saturdays.

The same goes for popular-music fandom, Marvel-movie fandom, *Star Wars* fandom, and *Star Trek* fandom (complete with costumes). And it goes for those who mock these things too, especially as they connect on social media. People seek out the place or the group where they feel they *belong*. Why?

Belonging provides a sense of identity, a context where we think, "I can really be *me*." We fit. We feel safe. We find comfort alongside those who share our opinions, interests, proclivities, animosity, or preferences. We find peace of mind in the familiar.

Sometimes we find belonging not so much in common interests but in a common cause. People identify with political parties, sometimes (sadly) rabidly. They believe the party will bring about change they long for or fend off change they fear. People throw themselves into efforts seeking to eradicate littering, climate change, homelessness, joblessness, or sex-trafficking—all worthy causes. Often such causes bring together people of varied backgrounds and yet the common cause offers a deep sense of belonging.

When we move to a new place, we often feel like we "don't belong" because the culture, rhythms, and patterns of life are new. It's unfamiliar. And sometimes, some long-time residents make it clear that they also think we "don't belong." Try being a Yankee in the American South. Or ask any immigrant.

A BROKEN SENSOR

So, although belonging is difficult to define, we know it when we feel it, even if the feeling is fleeting. Some nebulous combination of familiarity and shared experience makes us feel we belong. It is a delicious, easy, comfortable feeling—it is a little slice of heaven. This is why when we find it, we want to keep it, and we want to keep anything from changing in case it ruins it.

But then, almost inevitably, something shifts. Circumstances change. People come or go. Our sense of belonging begins to fade and we lose our grip on it. Now we find ourselves back searching for it again. For most of us, most of the time, this is not a desperate search or even a conscious one. It is more like a low-grade headache that we've learned to just live with. But sometimes the sense of "I don't belong" reaches migraine level and becomes a crisis. And for some people, this is how they live constantly: uncomfortable in their own skin or circumstances, dissatisfied with the life God has given them.

A fleeting sense of belonging, especially when it reaches that crisis point, will often lead us to question God. Is this really what he had in mind? Is this all he wants for my life? Frankly, those are good questions, and God has an answer for us: no. No, this is not all he has in mind or all he wants for us. Neither does he want us to keep searching for belonging in the same ways from the same sources.

When we feel that yearning for belonging it is because God created us to seek it and find it. Genesis 1 and 2 tell the story of how God created us to feel at home, to connect, to feel safe, to *belong* with him and in his creation. But Genesis 3 tells the story of Adam and Eve's rebellion against God, how sin entered the world through them, and how God rightly judged the world with a curse so that creation's relationship with him became broken. All of creation is affected by the curse. We no longer feel at home in this created world, and left to our own devices we can never find our way back to perfect belonging. Our sense of belonging is skewed. It's like a compass that doesn't point true north, so we end up searching for a good and God-designed thing in all the wrong places.

We were created for belonging. We yearn for belonging. But we find belonging to be, at least in any lasting way, elusive. So where does this leave us?

A NEW UNDERSTANDING OF BELONGING

What we need most is to understand belonging as God intends—to see it as he sees it. When we look for belonging in some vague coalescing of circumstances and people and feelings, we miss the mark because our hearts don't naturally turn to God's way. We want a good thing, a God-designed thing, but we instinctively look anywhere but to him. Instead of drifting from experience to place to social group, we need to understand belonging as part of God's design, as part of God's moral order, and as part of our identity, especially as Christians.

This is something you already understand, whether or not you realize it. If you have a loved one who has been in a serious car accident and suffered life-threatening injuries, they *belong* in the hospital. It's not where they want to be. They will be in a new and foreign place that is uncomfortable, surrounded by strangers. They will feel out of place and yearn to leave. But it is absolutely where they belong, so they can receive the care they need to survive and heal. It is *right* for them to be there.

And while they are there you *belong* at their side, at least as often as you are able. The hospital is just as uncomfortable and foreign to you. But it is *right* for you to be a comforting, stable presence in that environment where you feel out of place.

If you're a parent, you'll know that it's painfully common at some point of their childhood for our children to feel like they don't belong in our families, to feel like an outsider in their own gene pool and home. This is one of the most subtle, painful effects of the fall, that children would feel disconnected from those they were designed to love and be loved by. What do we tell our children when they feel this way? We tell them we love them. We tell them we're so grateful God gave them to this family on purpose and that he doesn't make mistakes. We reassure them that they *belong* because of God's good design and plan, and because they are loved and accepted in our family. They are part of us.

Belonging, then, is not defined by where we feel most comfortable, most at ease, or by where we have the most in common with others. Belonging is defined by where God intends us to be, and therefore where he intends us to find true life and deepest satisfaction and joy. It is a moral reality, a matter of what is right in God's eyes and what he calls us to. And it is a comforting reality, because doing what God has called us to means walking with him, living in his promises, and being in close relationship to him.

WHERE DO WE BELONG?

Belonging is never, almost by definition, discovered in isolation. Even the most introverted among us yearns to belong with others. We may not love crowds, but no one loves constant isolation. This is the way God made us; it was his idea. From the beginning he intended us to be in unhindered relationship with him and in unhindered relationship with each other. Sin fouled all that up, and continues to do so, but it is still God's intent that we *belong* with one another.

The Old Testament is essentially the story of God forming a people, a nation, for himself. It was supposed to be a community of people following God and walking closely with him. However, it's also the story of how they broke relationship with God and with one another, and the devastation that came each time they did this. And this is the story that sets up the coming of Jesus, that sets up the profound and undeniable need for a Savior, Redeemer, and Restorer.

As Christians, we know that Jesus came to die for our sins, to save us from judgment, and to restore our relationship with God. It is easy for us, especially in the West, to think of that individually—as in, Jesus saves *me* from *my* sins to restore *my* relationship with God. What we sometimes overlook is that Jesus also came to establish a kingdom, a community of believers who collectively follow him and represent him to the world. This is the kingdom to which all Christians *belong*. It is a kingdom of souls transformed from death to life, from bondage to sin to freedom in Christ. It is Christ's church, across the globe.

This is where we belong, to whom we belong. In fact, this is the truest reality of belonging: we belong to Christ as part of his church. And in his abundant care for us, as part of his plan to make himself known to the world, Christ designed his church to meet as local bodies of believers. (We see this in the book of Acts and throughout the epistles. We'll look at it further in the next chapter.) These are local churches, like the one you are part of (or are considering joining) and like the one where I pastor.

I said a few paragraphs ago that true belonging is both a moral reality and a comforting reality. Then I walked you through God's design, as shown in his word, for where you belong: the church. So this means that belonging to a church is both a morally good thing—something that God smiles on—and something that ought to bring comfort and joy, because it draws us closer to the heart of God. How does this work?

First, it means belonging isn't just passive. If something is morally good, something that God desires for us to do, then we have an obligation to act in obedience. So part of belonging is being purposeful and committed. Our tendency is always toward inertia, toward ease and passivity, but Hebrews 10:23-25 says:

> *Let us hold fast the confession of our hope without wavering, for he who promised is faithful. And let us consider how to stir up one another to love and good works, not neglecting to meet together, as is the habit of some, but encouraging one another, and all the more as you see the Day drawing near.*

Here is a clear call to take intentional action as part of the church—to stir one another up to love and good deeds, to not neglect meeting, and to encourage one another.

But note that the tone is not one of heavy-handedness. It's not a "do this, or else" tone: that would make church a place not of belonging but of burden. Rather it is a warm urging to build one another up. It is a command to do the things that make belonging both easier and richer. God has given us a clear direction, and by following it we find a clear reward. By obeying this command we are participating in welcoming others into belonging and in finding belonging ourselves.

Just as belonging is defined by obedience to God's summons (moral reality), it is defined by the promise and heart of Jesus too (comforting reality). In John 17, Jesus prays what is often known as the "High Priestly Prayer," in which he speaks to his Father on behalf of his disciples and the church through the ages—all those who would one day believe in him through the preaching of the gospel. (That's right, Jesus prayed for *you*!) In verses 20-26 he lays out his desires for his people through the ages:

I do not ask for these only, but also for those who will believe in me through their word, that they may all be one, just as you, Father, are in me, and I in you, that they also may be in us, so that the world may believe that you have sent me. The glory that you have given me I have given to them, that they may be one even as we are one, I in them and you in me, that they may become perfectly one, so that the world may know that you sent me and loved them even as you loved

*me. Father, I desire that they also, whom you have
given me, may be with me where I am, to see my glory
that you have given me because you loved me before
the foundation of the world. O righteous Father, even
though the world does not know you, I know you, and
these know that you have sent me. I made known to
them your name, and I will continue to make it known,
that the love with which you have loved me may be in
them, and I in them.*

Did you see what Jesus wants—what his heart for his
people is? He wants us to be *one*—that is, unified in him
in the same way that he is unified with his Father. This
isn't something we can just commit to and make happen
by best intentions and good hustle. But Jesus wouldn't
desire a thing for us that he doesn't also make available
to us. So there is a built-in promise here. This is a
supernatural kind of togetherness, given to believers by
the Holy Spirit. It is the kind of togetherness that isn't
defined by how we are similar to one another but rather
that overcomes differences the world around us might
see as insurmountable barriers. (Ephesians 2:11-22
explains and portrays this magnificently.) Jesus is
promising that his Spirit will reside in his church and be
our unifying, defining reality.

Jesus also makes clear that he wants us to know and
show his love; he wants us to be with him. He is offering
and promising a context of absolute, unhindered
belonging in and through himself. And it is not the

kind of belonging that is self-serving and exists solely so that we as individuals can have our needs met and find a place of comfort. Yes, the church is to be that, but it is to be that "so that the world may know that [God] sent [Jesus]." Our togetherness, our belonging, is to be a public evidence and invitation to the transforming, freeing, life-giving, comforting presence of Jesus Christ.

To belong, as God created us to belong, is so much more than finding a place of commonality or a comfort zone with those who share interests or oddities. It is more than gaining a level of comfort and familiarity. Certainly, those are wonderful discoveries and can spark significant friendships. But God made you and me for something even more than that. He made us to be members of his kingdom—of his church. Specifically, he made you to be part of a local body of believers. This is where and with whom you are meant to find belonging.

So we are to belong to a church because we are commanded to. And we are to belong to a church because it is good to. In the coming chapters we will look at what belonging to church means. We'll confront the challenges to belonging. Mostly, though, my hope is to help you see the beauty, life, and freedom of truly belonging to the body of Christ when it is truly exemplifying the character of Christ.

ACTION STEPS

- Consider your current perception or understanding of church membership. How does the reality of *belonging* fit with it? What might you need to reconsider or explore further?

- Where have you found a sense of belonging in the past or right now? What gave you that sense? Have you found it in a church?

- How has this chapter encouraged you to seek or deepen your belonging within your local church? What might you need to do, or change?

- If you struggle to grasp or accept the reality of belonging in a church, reflect on the lengths God went to to establish the church. Consider the way he established his people and kept his covenant with them in the Old Testament. Consider how he sent his Son to fulfill the covenant and establish the church in the New Testament. And consider the sacrifice Christ made to see his church formed.

- How are you going to think differently about church, or act differently toward your church, as a result of reading this chapter?

2. YOU BELONG

I hope you caught a glimpse in the previous chapter of how magnificent belonging can be in God's design and desire for us. You got a hint of the grandiosity and wonder of being part of God's kingdom. Hopefully it captured some part of you. But if we jump from all that wonder straight to "Ok, now go find belonging at a church" it could feel like receiving a brief pep talk before being told to climb Mount Everest. I don't want to offer you mere inspiration without a map or some instructions. That sort of vapid motivation tends to fizzle out fast and leave us frustrated, so my aim is to help you see where you are going and what God has in store for you.

When light hits a prism, it refracts into its different colors. What at first looks like a plain white beam of light is divided into a spectrum of beautiful components. That's similar to how the Bible describes the church. We read "church" and it sounds somewhat simple—a group of Christians who are organized with leaders, have some kind of formal structure, and meet regularly for the purpose of worshiping God. But that word "church" has a spectrum of beautiful components. Each one helps us see why and how we can belong. (And, as we go, I hope each will excite you to *want* to belong.)

THE CHURCH IS A FAMILY, AND YOU ARE ADOPTED INTO IT

One of the kindest things you can say about friends is that "they feel like family." It is a statement of trust, closeness, identity, and responsibility. When we describe friends this way we are reflecting something beautiful about God's design and desire for humanity, that familial relationships are meant to be near and dear to us. We were made to be part of a family.

We see this shown from the earliest pages of the Bible, where God made Adam and Eve *for* each other and commissioned them to be fruitful and multiply, that is, have a family. We see it when God tells Abraham that through his offspring all the nations of the earth would be blessed (Genesis 12:1-3). We see it when God establishes the people of Israel as twelve tribes, the offspring of twelve brothers (Genesis 49:1-28). The Bible uses familial language and descriptions throughout because they are the most foundational relational reality we have.

It also becomes clear throughout the Bible that God's idea of family extends far beyond biology. Someone else defines our closest, most meaningful relationships: Jesus

Christ. Jesus himself said, "Who are my mother and my brothers? ... Whoever does the will of God, he is my brother and sister and mother" (Mark 3:33, 35). When his disciples asked him to teach them to pray, Jesus said, "When you pray, say *Father*..." (Luke 11:2; my emphasis).

In these two brief exchanges, Jesus is expanding and defining what it truly means to be *family*. He points to those who faithfully walk with him and calls them his family. We know that Jesus is the Son of God, but he then points at his Father and tells us to talk to him as *our* Father.

Consider Romans 8:14-17:

> *For all who are led by the Spirit of God are sons of God. For you did not receive the spirit of slavery to fall back into fear, but you have received the Spirit of adoption as sons, by whom we cry, "Abba! Father!" The Spirit himself bears witness with our spirit that we are children of God, and if children, then heirs—heirs of God and fellow heirs with Christ, provided we suffer with him in order that we may also be glorified with him.*

All who believe in Christ have "received the Spirit of adoption as sons." We are children of God, and this is why Christ called us family. We are heirs with him. This changes everything about what it means to be in a family. For those with healthy, close families it lifts their eyes to an even greater reality. For those whose families are utterly dysfunctional, who are lonely, abandoned, orphaned, or divorced, it is a warm invitation into real family. In God's family, we share Christ's familial rights and standing in the eyes of God, and that means we will inherit the glories and riches of the heavenly kingdom.

But this family is not merely about a status or a right. It is about affection.

I know a few men and women who were adopted as children and legally became members of a family. They shared in the citizenship, the rights, and the last will and testament of their adoptive families. But some of them never received the love and affection that children should. Being adopted left them feeling like outsiders, like projects, like they didn't belong. This is not the case for believers in the family of God. Later in Romans 8 we read, "For I am sure that neither death nor life, nor angels nor rulers, nor things present nor things to come, nor powers, nor height nor depth, nor anything else in all creation, will be able to separate us from the love of God in Christ Jesus our Lord" (v 38-39). When we are adopted through the work of Jesus Christ into the family of God, we receive unconditional, immovable, eternal love as God's children. We could not be more loved. This is what adoption is *supposed* to look like.

Adoption and family are not mere metaphors to help us understand how we relate as Christians. The Bible doesn't say we are *like* a family; it says we *are* family. Receiving the Holy Spirit transforms us, we become new people, and that means we are no longer strangers, enemies, or rivals.

We are brothers and sisters in *Christ*. We are children *of God*. Mark 10:29-30 explains what that means for us:

> Jesus said, "Truly, I say to you, there is no one who has left house or brothers or sisters or mother or father or children or lands, for my sake and for the gospel, who will not receive a hundredfold now in this time, houses and brothers and sisters and mothers and children and lands, with persecutions, and in the age to come eternal life."

Belonging to the family of God is not just an identity change—it comes with a promise. Even if following Jesus separated you from your family of origin (and following Jesus can be that costly) or if you do not have family with whom you are close, in the church you gain a family exponentially, what Jesus called "a hundredfold." You become part of a family marked by the sacrifice and humility and love of Jesus Christ. We get it wrong often. We sin against one another. We hurt one another. But, as my friend Sam Allberry reminds us, "The blood of Jesus is thicker than the blood of biology." We have the unfailing love of God, proven by the sacrifice of Jesus, so we can freely repent and be forgiven and grow with one another as children of God. In Christ, we belong to a new and eternal family.

THE CHURCH IS A BODY, AND YOU NEED IT (AND IT NEEDS YOU)

We commonly see the word "body" being used to mean a corporate gathering, a collective of people coming together for a cause or purpose, such as a "voting body." Sometimes it is used simply to mean the majority portion of a group: "The main body of protestors marched down Main Street while a small number broke off and proceeded up First Avenue." But when we call the church the "body of Christ" we mean much more than this.

In 1 Corinthians 12, describing the church, Paul says, "The body is one and has many members, and all the members of the body, though many, are one body, so it is with Christ. For in one Spirit we were all baptized into one body ... For the body does not consist of one member but of many" (v 12-14). When you first read this, it's easy to think in terms of "member of an organization," but the following verses, 15-27, make clear what Paul means. He is writing about a physical body.

This complex metaphor opens our eyes to deeper spiritual and relational realities. Paul writes about how the foot cannot feel excluded from the body because it is not a hand (v 15). It is exactly what God intended it to be, it plays its particular purpose in the life of the body, and it is essential. Then Paul writes that the eye cannot exclude the hand from the body because it has no need of it (v 21), but rather that all the parts of the body are indispensable and worthy of honor.

This is an image of perfect design, with no extraneous parts, no useless parts, and no unwanted parts. All the parts of the body belong. God put together the body with intentionality, and he does the same with his church. We often "do church" in a way that leaves people feeling useless or inferior (or feeling powerful and superior). But that is not God's intent. Every part of the body needs the others, both the greater and the lesser.

The implications of this are enormous. In a physical body if there is disunity, animosity, or infighting we call that *illness*, like a cancer or an autoimmune disease. If a church is marked by disunity, animosity, or infighting it is just as ill and cancerous. As members, we are called to honor one another, support one another, and play the part God has given us so the whole body thrives.

If a body part (what the Bible calls a "member") is cut off, it will shrivel and rot because it is separated from its life source. It must be skillfully, carefully, and gently reattached and the body must accept it back for it to heal and the body to be whole. The same is true for you and me. If we are cut off from the church, we will spiritually shrivel up and die. We need to be reattached to the body of Christ and we need the body to accept us back. We need the life of the body, the lifeblood of fellowship in Christ and teaching in the word.

Unlike the amputation of a hand or a toe or an ear, which is forcibly done by someone else, we often voluntarily amputate ourselves from the church. Sometimes Christians decide, for whatever reason, to cut themselves off. Sometimes they drift into it. In this sense we are different from a human body—for while a human body may not always work properly, it generally stays put together. A church body needs its members to deliberately and consciously stay connected, to circulate life, to support one another.

The metaphor of the body eliminates one of our problematic human tendencies: being parasitic. The parts of a body depend on one another, mutually. Sometimes one is weaker and needs to be restored and supported by others—think of broken bones or surgically-repaired organs. But no body part is designed to suck the life and energy out of the others, to draw on the life-source without sharing in the giving of life too. We are to give as well as gain—and it's as we give that we most gain. This is what Romans 12:5 calls being "one body in Christ, and individually members one of another." *We are members of one another*. How beautiful. What a high calling. And what hope, because we are *in Christ*. Left to ourselves we amputate, we become cancer, we are parasites. But, made new in Christ, we belong to one another as sharers of Christ's love and life.

THE CHURCH IS A BUILDING, AND YOU ARE A BRICK IN THE WALL

When some Christians hear that "the church is a building" their immediate response is "No, the church is the people." I wholeheartedly agree, in one sense, and yet I also disagree in another. Your church is a building? Let's look at Ephesians 2:19-22 to better understand.

So then you are no longer strangers and aliens, but you are fellow citizens with the saints and members of the household of God, built on the foundation of the apostles and prophets, Christ Jesus himself being the cornerstone, in whom the whole structure, being joined together, grows into a holy temple in the Lord. In him you also are being built together into a dwelling place for God by the Spirit.

This passage starts by addressing the people as citizens and saints, members of a household. That is the language of human rights, of responsibility, of relationship, and of family. But then Paul changes the imagery and begins describing a structure being built. He is not describing a physical church building, but rather the body of believers who are the structure. Whereas the descriptions of the church as a family or a body are organic and alive, this architectural picture here in Ephesians is vital for us to understand because it shows the right order of the church—the blueprint, if you will—and it shows clearly who the architect and designer is.

The church is built on the foundation of Scripture and the cornerstone of Jesus Christ. When it says, "apostles and prophets" it means those who carried the explicit authority of God and spoke his words to the people: that is, the ones who gave us the Bible. That means that their words all pointed to Jesus and depend on Jesus, so he is the cornerstone on which the whole church rests.

This church, with Christ as the cornerstone, is designed and built by God. He is the architect and builder. No one else can take credit for the life of the church, the success of the church, the sustaining of the church, or the growth of the church. It grows "in the Lord." This is not mechanical growth, but rather the powerful presence of God bringing spiritual life to this body of believers.

When we read "growth" we almost inevitably think of size or numbers. We have an entire industry built around "church growth" after all. But that is not the way that growth is depicted here. We are "being built together into a dwelling place for God by the Spirit." This supernatural structure that God is building us into, and building up through us, is dwelled in by his Spirit. He is making his home with his people in his church. Growth, then, should be defined as an increase of the reality and presence of God in our midst.

To be part of the church means to be part of this structure, a brick in the wall of the dwelling place of God. It means we, along with all the other bricks and joists and studs and rafters, rest on the foundation of God's word fulfilled in Jesus Christ. We belong to the house of God.

THE CHURCH IS GOD'S PLAN, AND YOU ARE PART OF IT

I mentioned in chapter 1 that most of us are not moved to a sense of belonging by being part of some grand

Belong

plan or strategy. Being told that "you are a cog in the machine" or even that "you play a key role" is not very warm or welcoming. What I hope you see now is that God's plan is not coldly strategic or mechanical. It is relational, loving, full of heart and life, and designed for closeness. Being part of a plan or mission with those we love is an entirely different story and a context of profound belonging.

Acts 1 – 4 tells the story of how God's church was formed and then set out on God's mission. In Acts 1:8, just before ascending to heaven, Jesus tells his followers, "But you will receive power when the Holy Spirit has come upon you, and you will be my witnesses in Jerusalem and in all Judea and Samaria, and to the end of the earth." This is the mission of the church. It is also the identity of the believer, and the most encouraging part is that it is built on the promise of the presence and power of Christ through the Holy Spirit.

We go on to read the story of Pentecost, when the Holy Spirit came with power and thousands of people were "added to their number" (2:41, NIV). We read of the miraculous boldness of the disciples, despite lacking education and societal status, to preach and proclaim. We read of miracles displaying the power of the Holy Spirit and the presence of Christ. And we read of the church's beautiful unity as they studied the Scriptures, learned from the apostles, and shared whatever they had to care for one another (v 42-47).

We also read of persecution and opposition as the apostles were arrested and threatened by the religious and governmental rulers. In Acts 4 Peter and John are hauled before the counsel of rulers in Jerusalem. There they boldly proclaim Jesus as Savior. They are released with a command to be silent and never preach the gospel of Jesus again. In response they go straight to their fellow believers, the church, and pray together not for comfort or safety but for *boldness* to continue declaring Jesus Christ and for God to continue to work with power: "And when they had prayed, the place in which they were gathered together was shaken, and they were all filled with the Holy Spirit and continued to speak the word of God with boldness" (4:31).

This prayer sets the stage for the mission Jesus gave them to be fulfilled, but maybe not in the way we would anticipate. When we think of fulfilling a mission it's easy to picture James Bond or Seal Team 6 or Black Widow carrying out a bold, strategic, decisive action, ideally with a bit of flare and drama. So we might naturally assume that God raised up an army of impressive commando-level missionaries to carry the gospel to the ends of the earth with courageous fervor. Instead the following verses say this:

Now the full number of those who believed were of one heart and soul, and no one said that any of the things that belonged to him was his own, but they had everything in common. And with great power the

apostles were giving their testimony to the resurrection
of the Lord Jesus, and great grace was upon them all.
There was not a needy person among them, for as
many as were owners of lands or houses sold them and
brought the proceeds of what was sold and laid it at the
apostles' feet, and it was distributed to each as any had
need. (4:32-35)

It was not simply fervor and intensity that carried the mission forward. It was boldness in the gospel *marked by* unity in Christ, being of "one heart and soul." It wasn't a frenzied, loud, bombastic boldness but the kind of boldness that gives courage to sacrifice for the sake of others and ultimately for the sake of Jesus. And that is what happened, starting with the martyrdom of Stephen and the conversion of Paul which led to the gospel being taken to the ends of the earth. God's plan was fulfilled through his unified, faithful, bold church, not by a collection of lone rangers. And the church in Acts is the same church to which you belong today.

GOD'S LIGHT TO THE WORLD
At the beginning of this chapter I compared the Bible's descriptions of the church to a prism which refracts lights into the full spectrum of beauty. That analogy works from a descriptive standpoint, but also in terms of identity. The church is God's light to the world, shining the beauty of Jesus and the truth of the gospel to those around us. And we need each facet of the light in order for people to find their place of belonging. We must

be a family, adopted and united in the love of God. We must be a body which has no useless or extraneous parts but rather honoring and supporting and depending on each member. We must be a building, a dwelling place for the presence of God with Jesus as our cornerstone. And we must be the fulfillment of God's plan as we rely on the Holy Spirit for boldness, courage, selflessness, and generosity. If any of these is missing, the church is lacking. But if each is present, the church is the one environment in which every person can find the belonging God intended.

NEXT SUNDAY

What might it feel like to walk into church next Sunday with these realities in mind? Instead of encountering greeters, coffee servers, acquaintances, and strangers, you encounter family members. Instead of old people, young people, and peers, you encounter fathers and mothers, uncles and aunts, cousins, nephews and nieces, brothers and sisters. Even if you are brand new to a church, if you are a Christian, this is your reality in Christ.

When you serve, or when you see people serving, that is no longer filling out a volunteer roster or doing a duty; you are a body part supporting and assisting the health of the whole body. When you hear someone's prayer request about a job search or an illness, no longer is that a distant burden that means little to you; it is the weight being carried by an appendage of your body. When you see someone raise their hands in worship and another drop to their knees in prayer, this is your body healing and being restored, so you can rejoice with them.

As you look around your church and consider all the uniqueness, the individuals, and the stories represented by the people there, you can marvel at God's work. He built that house using those materials. He joined that ragtag, oddball bunch, including you, together by the power of the Holy Spirit, and he is executing his plan to make Jesus known to the world through you all.

You belong to a miraculous family and body and house. You are on a mission of eternal significance. There is nothing mundane or trite about church. It is God's design and purpose and home for every believer, and you belong.

ACTION STEPS

- Which of the biblical pictures of church explored in this chapter particularly resonated with you or encouraged you to belong? Do you need to shift your view in any way? Reflect on the truths of Scripture, laid out in definitive statements in this chapter, about who you are. Remember that who God says you are and who he designed you to be are far more real than how you perceive yourself.

- When the church feels like a dysfunctional family—and it definitely does sometimes— focus on what Christ has called *you* to. Even when others in the church are not acting as a loving family, you can love them, serve them, pray for them, bear with them. Rather than letting the dysfunction make you feel like an outsider, be the family of God for them even when they are not modelling love to you.

- When and how do you feel the temptation to drift toward amputation from the body of Christ? Examine yourself to be aware of those temptations and tendencies, especially because they are usually passive and quiet. Then consider what steps you can take to resist that drift and to maintain close connection to the church.

- Consider what it means to be the dwelling place of God. Now consider what it means to be part of God's plan to save the world. Those are easy sentences to say, but they are world-changing, life-defining realities. How do they adjust your view of church? How do they change your desire or passion to be part of the church?

3. WHAT DOES IT LOOK LIKE TO BELONG?

At some level, I knew the big, beautiful realities of chapters 1 and 2 before I ever experienced them in an actual real church. I could have written a "philosophy of ministry" paper or taught a seminar on "healthy church culture" to articulate them. But that is a far cry from finding a church *home*, from feeling like I truly *belonged* to a local body. The doctrine of the church—the theology—needs to be embodied for it to truly matter.

As I wrote in the preface, there was a time not so many years ago when I was weary and jaded toward church, but even then, I could have given you a lengthy checklist of what a healthy church should look like. What I had come to realize, though, was that a checklist doesn't create belonging. A church could have great preaching, powerful music, top-notch children's ministry, and an airtight discipleship program and it still not be a true family or a healthy body. For the weary and wary, pristine ministry programming isn't the answer. Culture is.

Culture, much like belonging, is one of those words that is easier to sense than to define. But here is my best attempt at a definition: culture is the collection of actions, reactions, vocabulary, attitude, and perspective that expresses the norm for a particular group of people. Basically, culture is how a group of people instinctively, naturally act toward one another and how they interact with outsiders. For a church the implications of this are enormous. If everything in a church's structure and teaching and programming is rock solid, but the culture is cold or judgmental, it isn't a welcoming place.

The proclamation of the gospel of Jesus Christ is the foundation on which any real church is built. A church *cannot* be healthy without biblically grounded, gospel-shaped preaching and teaching. But a church can have this kind of preaching and still be unhealthy. As sinners, we have the unfortunate and hurtful ability to be profoundly hypocritical, meaning that we can both proclaim and hear a gospel of grace and still not be shaped by it or share it. When that happens, our church culture actually undermines and contradicts what is preached.

On the other (and better) hand, our church culture can embody the truths of the gospel in a way that brings them to life, creating a different kind of environment and reality than anything that can be found anywhere else. The kind of culture that offers deep, biblical belonging can only be created by the transforming work of the Holy

Spirit in the lives of individuals and the corporate life of the body. At Immanuel Church, where I serve, we call this "gospel culture" because we are very creative.[1] This is what the church is *for*; it's our purpose. It is enormous and miraculous, but it is also mundane and granular. It is beyond our comprehension, but it is tangible in our day-to-day rhythms, interactions, and priorities. It is difficult to articulate and explain in full, but it is easily recognizable when we find it, and it is a joy to belong to it and contribute to it when we do. Just as we know a tree by its fruit, so we know this beautiful, profound gospel culture by what it produces.

In this chapter, I am going to walk through some essential aspects of this kind of church culture. This isn't an ordered list or a step-by-step process. It's more like a collection of ingredients that make up the secret sauce of gospel culture, or a color palette to be blended in hues that paint a beautiful gospel culture.

COME AS YOU ARE, BUT DON'T STAY THAT WAY

Few things make someone feel less like they belong than being judged. Most churches don't wear their judgment

---

1 I would be remiss and borderline dishonest to write at length about "gospel culture" without giving credit where it is due. I did not come up with this name or this idea. Ray Ortlund Jr., the founding pastor of Immanuel Church, wrote a book titled *The Gospel* (Crossway Books, 2014) that is foundational in how I understand the gospel's shaping of the life of the body. Even he would say that it was a discovery over time rather than a formula he developed. Gospel culture has become a defining reality for us as a church. This chapter is my attempt to divide this miraculous thing into its ingredients to help you understand and recognize it so that you can contribute to growing it.

like a jersey. Instead it comes out more subtly—that head-to-toe evaluating look, the raised eyebrow and intake of breath when you share some part of your story, or the comments of how "*We* do things *this* way at *our* church." We all know what this feels like—that sense of being looked down on or that it is unsafe to share what you really struggle with or what is truly going on in your life.

Isn't this antithetical to what a church ought to be like, though? A culture that embodies the free grace, mercy, and transformed life offered in the gospel will welcome and embrace people in any state of soul or life. After all, Jesus was known as a friend of sinners (Matthew 9:11, 11:16-19). Granted, this was a title bestowed on him as an insult by those who thought they were upholding the purity of the religious law. They failed to realize their slight was a magnificently accurate description of our Savior's heart, and they failed to recognize their own need for such a friend. In the same way "friend of sinners" described Jesus, it describes a church truly shaped by his gospel.

Jesus made "tax collectors and sinners" (Matthew 9:11), known as the moral outcasts of his day, feel safe around him. He invited himself into their houses and welcomed them wherever he was. His presence made the least likely, the undesirable, and the shame-filled people yearn to be near him. Followers of Jesus, his church, are called to extend the same welcome and grace. To do this we need to remember that we *are* the tax collectors and sinners, the moral outcasts. Romans tells us that "none is righteous, no, not one," and "all have sinned and fall short of the glory of God" (3:10, 23). So a healthy church culture does not invite people in because we have it all together. We invite people in because Jesus has put us back together. We say, "Come as you are, and find what you need *in Jesus*, as I did."

When we encounter this sort of welcome at a church it feels good, but it might spark suspicion too. Being told to "come as you are" is great, but it often sounds either like a church with no biblical standards ("You're just fine as you are") or the bait in a looming bait-and-switch. Does this church take the Bible seriously or are they soft-pedaling biblical moral standards? Or are they just luring me in with faux kindness so they can drop the moral hammer on me later?

These are fair questions, especially given the range of negative experiences you may have had at churches. Again we get to look to Jesus as we seek answers. Think about his disciples: an odd group of young men from different socioeconomic backgrounds, with different political inclinations and different amounts of biblical and moral training. Time and again we see them reveal their immaturity, foolishness, and basic misunderstanding of who Jesus actually is. They argued about who will be the greatest (Mark 9:33-34). They tried to shoo little children away from Jesus (10:13-16). They told Jesus to stop talking about dying (8:31-33). In his final hours they betrayed him, denied him, and abandoned him (14:1-11, 48-50, 66-72). And yet he went to the cross for them and then sent his Holy Spirit to empower them to launch the very church we are part of today.

Jesus is patient. His Father is "slow to anger, and abounding in steadfast love" (Exodus 34:6). So the invitation to "come as you are" is neither a casual shrug about sins and struggles, nor a veiled threat. It is a welcome into the same patience God shows us. Nobody changes quickly, at least not in our souls. And God knows this. We find belonging in the church when we are welcomed into the body of Christ carrying with us every difficult, ugly, sinful, broken, traumatized, quirky, frustrating thing in our lives and are told, "We're glad you're here; let's walk in friendship with Jesus together." And we welcome others into belonging when we fold them into the loving, patient, transforming friendship of Jesus.

BRING YOUR NEED AND MEET A NEED

"How are you doing?"

"Fine, you?"

How many times a week do you have some variation of this conversation? Maybe you answer with "Good" or "Better than I deserve" (if you are particularly pious) or "Tired" (if you are a modern adult). Whichever it is, to call it a conversation is a bit generous. It's more like an instinctive polite social ritual. The first line isn't really a question and the second line isn't really an answer.

Because truly answering the question, "How are you doing?" can be terrifying. (And to receive an honest answer would be jarring, to say the least.)

Honest answers would often look more like "Lonely," "Addicted to porn," "Depressed," "Aimless and not really sure where my life is going," "Frustrated in my marriage," "Distant from God," or "Ashamed." But how could you ever look someone in the eye and reveal such things about yourself? To be that honest would be terrifying. It would expose the darkest, most sensitive parts of your life.

Exactly. And that is precisely how Christ calls you and me to relate to others in our church.

"Those who are well have no need of a physician, but those who are sick. I came not to call the righteous, but sinners." These words from Jesus in Mark 2:17 are an invitation to bring our need. Jesus is not excluding people from his care and from salvation. He is pointing out that some people exclude themselves. Who is so righteous that they do not need Christ? Nobody. But some people think they are. They hide their sins and failures and needs, or they deny them altogether. So Jesus can do nothing for them.

But if we bring those needs to Jesus in the way a sick person lays out their pain and symptoms to a doctor, he can heal us. Jesus is inviting us to total honesty—to humbly expose what is really going on in our lives. It is a distinct line Jesus is asking us to cross. If we withhold our need from Christ, we are withholding ourselves from wholeness and healing, and maybe even from salvation. "But if we walk in the light, as he is in the light, we have fellowship with one another, and the blood of Jesus his Son cleanses us from all sin" (1 John 1:7). True honesty—moving from the darkness of withdrawal and withholding into the light of Christ—moves us into true belonging. We encounter the healing of Jesus Christ as he cleanses us from the filth and infection of sin and we encounter joyful unity with other Christians who have also entered the light.

When we see a doctor we have confidence that it is safe to tell them everything, even the potentially embarrassing stuff. It isn't always easy to say, but we know it's the right context and we know the doctor will better diagnose and prescribe treatment if he has all the information. In the same way, the church is where God intends for Jesus to do his work. We "walk in the light" and he cleanses and heals, most often *through* the care of our fellow believers as we "confess [our] sins to one another and pray for one another, that [we] may be healed" (James 5:16).

The first time I encountered this invitation to total honesty and walking in the light in a men's Bible study I was, dare I say, skeptical. To be more accurate, I thought it sounded like total pie-in-the-sky nonsense. It felt like an invitation for people to gawk at my embarrassment, give me unwanted advice, and gossip about me later. It simply did not feel like an invitation into safety and healing. But I failed to understand something fundamental about the gospel of Jesus Christ: when people truly throw themselves on the mercy of Jesus, they are transformed and become conduits of his mercy and healing to others. So inviting me to be truly honest wasn't a threat but an invitation to healing and burden lifting.

Here is how that works.

First, being transformed means going from dead in sin to alive in Jesus. It does not mean being elevated above those who have yet to give their lives to Jesus.

When a fellow Christian comes to us and takes the risk of total honesty about sin, about pain, about shame, or about anything else that is dark in their lives our response must be "Me too, thank you for telling me." Even if we haven't experienced the exact same things, we know the experience of bringing burdens to Jesus and finding the freedom only he can offer. We are not above that honest person; we are *with them*. There is no room for ego or hierarchy or smugness in the family of God. People feel safe when other believers say "Me too" rather than "Oh my" or "Are you serious?"

Second, experiencing the freedom of forgiveness and cleansing means we want others to experience the same thing through Christ.

If you have a friend who has benefited from a chiropractor, you absolutely know it—because every time you mention the slightest ailment, they recommend him. While this can induce the occasional eye roll, what it really shows is that they've experienced significant help and healing and want you to experience the same. They have confidence that their chiropractor can help whatever it is that's hurting you. This is how we should be in the church; we can be confident that Jesus can heal whatever struggles people have and we should want to share the healing gospel balm we have ourselves experienced.

When someone begins to feel the safety of a church culture shaped by the gospel and they take the risk of being honest, what is our response? It cannot be: "Here are five steps you can take to fix that problem" or "Let me recommend a great book that could help." Those might be helpful at some point, but we are not the physician. We don't do the healing. We are patients too. We need Jesus, so what we must do is walk in the light *with* our brothers and sisters to the very feet of Jesus. We lift their needs and burdens and confessions up to Jesus with them, just as we need others to do for us.

Of course we may advise them to seek further pastoral help, or counsel them to make practical changes—but first and foremost, we keep inviting them to take their struggles to Jesus and let Jesus help and heal.

Third, Christ transforms how we see other people and it opens our eyes to who they really are: image-bearers of God, worthy of dignity and honor.

C.S. Lewis famously wrote that "there are no ordinary people. You have never talked to a mere mortal." We only recognize this when Christ has lifted our eyes from our natural temporal, navel-gazing perspective to his magnificent eternal perspective. Every person you encounter in your church is an eternal image-bearer of God, imbued with profound dignity and worth. Every believer you meet is his beloved child.

Most of us do not recognize that about ourselves or others. We see ourselves as defined either by our worst moments or by what we deem to be our greatest accomplishments (in which case, a bad moment can bring us crashing down). We do not naturally see one another as defined by our Creator—this only happens when Jesus opens our eyes. Until this happens we cannot feel safe around others, we cannot be fully honest, and we cannot offer safety to others. If we were to reveal what is deep inside us it might be exploited, used, turned against us, or neglected. However, once Jesus gets hold of us, and we see ourselves and others as beloved and dignified and of more worth than we can imagine, we treat them as they deserve. We protect and uphold one another's dignity, so there is no room for shaming or gossip or harsh criticism. And we "outdo one another in showing honor" (Romans 12:10) by intentionally, publicly, verbally highlighting and celebrating how we see God's fingerprints on the lives of those around us and by reminding people of who they are in Christ.

BEAR WITH ONE ANOTHER

I'm old enough now to have had most of my idealism knocked off. Live enough life and, unless you abide in the spirit of Buddy the elf, you will learn not to assume that every human interaction and relationship will be the start of a new best friendship. To put a finer point on it, you learn that people can really frustrate and hurt other people. The Bible is very, very realistic about this, including within a church.

So how do we create a culture of safety and unity in Christ if we will inevitably run into, and cause, conflicts? Paul lays it out like this in Ephesians 4:1-3: "I therefore, a prisoner for the Lord, urge you to walk in a manner worthy of the calling to which you have been called, with all humility and gentleness, with patience, bearing with one another in love, eager to maintain the unity of the Spirit in the bond of peace." This is a clear call to unity, but it is not a description of some Zen-like state, absent of any friction or conflict or disagreement. Rather it *assumes* that friction and disagreement will exist—that's why Paul doesn't just say to *walk in gentleness and love*, but instead calls us to patiently bear with one another. We only need patience when we are being tested and we only need to bear with people who are frustrating us.

Lest we slip into accidental-victim mode, remember that we drive others crazy and need them to gently, patiently bear with us too. We tend to excel at noticing and recalling all the ways we bear with others, while completely missing the ways they have borne with us.

In these verses Paul is calling us to mutual bearing-with for the sake of unity in the gospel. None of us will find a home or place of belonging in our church without others patiently, gently bearing with our ignorance, our bad habits, our differing theological viewpoints, and our varying preferences. Equally, we cannot hope others will find a home unless we see them with enough love to show them the same patience.

1 Corinthians 13 is, famously, "the love chapter" of the Bible. Because we in the West usually equate love to romance, it is most often heard as part of a wedding homily. While there is some application there, this is in fact a chapter about Christian love within the body of Christ. And it says this: "Love bears all things, believes all things, hopes all things, endures all things" (v 7). To rephrase and expound upon this, Christian love between believers is shown by bearing with others, thinking the best of them, seeing their bright future in Christ, and walking with them patiently toward that bright future. This is what Paul is calling us to in Ephesians 4 too, so that we "maintain the unity of the Spirit in the bond of peace."

These passages are so freeing and so intimidating. They are freeing because they show that unity in the church is not found in unanimity. Safety and belonging are not found in fitting in just right or finding a group of people exactly like us. Our calling as followers of Jesus is not to agree with everyone or get everyone to agree with us. It's not to be best friends with everyone. And it's not to see every aspect of life the same way as everyone else. Which brings us to why these are intimidating passages.

Our calling as followers of Jesus is to be so shaped by love that we patiently bear with and walk alongside others *despite* our differences. This is what makes the body of Christ a miracle, and it is something we can only discover and live out by the work of the Holy Spirit in our lives. This is how we offer safety and belonging to others and how we find it ourselves. We love our neighbors as ourselves by bearing with them as we would have them bear with us.

CHRISTIAN FELLOWSHIP, FOR REAL

Like most American churches of its era, the church I grew up in had a fellowship hall. This was the taupe room with drop ceilings furnished with eight-person round tables and metal folding chairs. It hosted myriad events from Bible studies to meals to business meetings. It is where I would most often pilfer baked goods from the old folks' Sunday-school class or get yelled at for running in church. In my memory it is a mix of green-bean casserole, coffee cake, pungent perfume, rug burn, and a lot of Bible. So, for better or worse, that's what I associate the word "fellowship" with.

Christian fellowship—what we are invited into in the church—is so much more than that. It is more than gathering, more than socializing, more than studying.

But it is not less. We can't have fellowship without gathering. It works best when there is meaningful relational connection. And it must be centered on the truths and realities of Scripture. But what *is* it, and why is it so essential for truly belonging to a church?

A simple way to define Christian fellowship is a gathering of believers where the Bible's one-another commands are lived out with joy. Here's a non-comprehensive list of these commands:

- Love one another. (John 13:34)

- Build one another up. (1 Thessalonians 5:11)

- Bear with one another. (Colossians 3:13)

- Forgive one another. (Ephesians 4:32)

- Serve one another. (Galatians 5:13)

- Be devoted to one another. (Romans 12:10, NIV)

- Pray for one another. (James 5:16)

- Teach one another. (Colossians 3:16)

- Live in harmony with one another. (Romans 12:16)

- Submit to one another. (Ephesians 5:21)

- Honor one another. (Romans 12:10)

- Welcome one another. (Romans 15:7)

- Encourage one another. (1 Thessalonians 4:18)

- Exhort one another. (Hebrews 3:13)

Imagine being in a group of Christians who, transformed by Jesus, interacted this way. It's hard to imagine *not* belonging, right? It would be the most uplifting, Christ-centered, happy, unified group of people. And that is precisely Christ's design for his church.

Consider two verses from the New Testament about fellowship.

But if we walk in the light, as he is in the light, we have fellowship with one another, and the blood of Jesus his Son cleanses us from all sin. (1 John 1:7)

We looked at this verse earlier, but it is well worth more examination. It shows the source of our fellowship and the kind of fellowship it is. The source is the cleansing of Jesus as we step out of the imprisonment and isolation of sin. This kind of fellowship is free, unhindered, not looking over our shoulders for the threat. In Christ, our fellowship together is defined by honesty, safety, freedom, and unhindered, unhampered happiness.

And they devoted themselves to the apostles' teaching and the fellowship, to the breaking of bread and the prayers. (Acts 2:42)

When the Holy Spirit first formed the church in Jerusalem and they were first gathering, this is what it looked like. This is what the Spirit moved God's people to do. They *devoted* themselves to the teaching of the gospel "and the fellowship." That means the gathering of believers was in order to build one another up in Christ. It was intentional and prioritized. It did not just happen. They threw themselves into it for the sake of closeness, growth, and one-anothering.

It is the same today. Christian fellowship doesn't just happen. We have an impressive but sad ability to gather together and yet fail at meaningful fellowship. We can even study the Bible and miss out on it. But if we are intent on trusting Christ to work in us as we gather, and are open to being Christ-like as we gather, then— whether it's for a meal or a church service or a golf game or a playdate for the kids—we share in that beautiful fellowship. We too can one-another like the early church and experience the unity, connection, and joy of true Christian fellowship. We were designed for this kind of fellowship, this kind of connection in Jesus, and we cannot find it anywhere but in the body of Christ.

COMMITMENT DOESN'T HAVE TO BE SCARY

In chapter 1 we saw that "belonging" means more than just feeling at home or at ease. We *belong* when we are fulfilling the design God has given us and living as he made us to live. And he made us to be part of his church, to find a place of honesty and safety and patience and healing and fellowship. But we will not always feel like we belong. Church will not always go smoothly, either because of something awry in our hearts, or because of something awry in the body of believers, or maybe because of both.

When we feel like we don't belong, we often live with a foot out the door and an eye on other possibilities. We hold back relationally, and we hold back our gifts, talents, and resources (or we give them elsewhere, in the places we have decided we more truly belong). We give less to the church and are unable to receive as much too. That, of course, becomes a self-perpetuating negative cycle: holding back means we feel like we belong less, so we hold back more, and so we feel we belong less... Here's the stark reality: you can never truly find belonging at a church unless you commit yourself to it.

Commitment to a church can sound intimidating and risky, especially if you have been hurt in church before. But think about the marks of belonging we have looked at—a culture shaped by the gospel, a culture of safety, honesty, patience, bearing with one another; a place of true fellowship. Committing yourself to that is giving yourself to the best possible environment for your flourishing.

BUILDING WHAT YOU'D LOVE TO SEE

You may be thinking, "But my church doesn't look very much like this gospel culture" or asking yourself how someone even begins to see this kind of culture in a church. The short answer is to start small and with intentional steps. Gather some folks from your church family, talk and pray through these ingredients of gospel culture, and commit to them. It isn't up to you to change your church; that is up to God. It is up to you to "commit your way to the LORD [and] trust in him, and he will act." (Psalm 37:5).

Remember, Hebrews 10:24-25 says, "And let us consider how to stir up one another to love and good works, not neglecting to meet together, as is the habit of some, but encouraging one another, and all the more as you see the Day drawing near." I used to read this as a sort of measuring stick or threat. I needed to grit my teeth and keep trudging through the church doors or else bad things would happen. But that's not what it says at all. *Why* does it says not to cease meeting? So that we can be *encouraged*. We gather together for encouragement, for being stirred up to love and good deeds. When we commit ourselves to being part of a church, and when we commit to pursuing and contributing to a gospel culture that reflects gospel teaching, we are throwing ourselves into the very heart of Christ—love, good deeds, encouragement. You cannot find true belonging anywhere else—and why would you want to?

ACTION STEPS

- Do you have a checklist of what you're looking for in a church? Does the list reflect "healthy church culture"? Consider how good doctrine, good programs, good music, and even good teaching/preaching can be undermined by an unhealthy church culture. How have you seen this happen in churches? And how have you experienced the opposite—a healthy gospel culture regardless of the music, resources, or programs?

- How have you experienced the freedom and transformational power of biblical honesty, honor, and safety in church? How can you intentionally extend these things to others in your church and participate in a gospel culture?

- Imagine a church community that lives out the "one another" commands. What would that look like? What would that feel like to be part of? Draw up a list of three or four practical and specific things you are going to start doing that will increase or catalyze the "one anothering" within your church.

- Commitment to a church can be intimidating. What might make you hesitate to commit yourself to a church? What are the costs of holding back? How can you take the next step of commitment at your church?

4. UNITY: THE ONLY WAY BELONGING HAPPENS

A body whose parts are not working together is sick. A family that is fractured is dysfunctional. A building that is cracking and crumbling is unsafe and in need of either renovation or condemnation. These are the metaphors and images we saw earlier that Scripture uses for the church, and it's easy to see why unity is essential in any church if people are to find a place of belonging. Unity is proof of health and solidity—evidence that a local church is a community of believers worthy of our commitment.

We tend to gravitate toward easy "unity" in the same way we gravitate toward easy belonging (as we saw in chapter 1). We want unity to just click, to come easily. We want it to "just feel right" and be "natural," by which we usually mean we want it to take little effort. Our instinctive assumption is that being unified to other people, especially Christians, will happen by proximity and shouldn't be too difficult or take too much time.

Because of these assumptions we are often attracted to one of two kinds of church community that appear unified but actually undermine the very thing.

THE FACADE OF FRIENDLY UNITY

There's an unignorable fact about Southern culture in America: Southerners are *nice*—pathologically, call-you-honey, back-slapping, stop-by-any-time nice. Aside from the occasional over-testosteroned and overcompensating young man in a jacked-up pickup, you would be hard pressed to find a more pleasant and polite context. In the Midwest, where I grew up, though people were less warm and more stolid, you could count on them as neighbors. They sought to ruffle no feathers and expected the same in return.

In both contexts, this same outward niceness pervades the church. People don't argue. Controversial topics are avoided in conversation and from the pulpit. Sins are not often confessed to; that would cause a stir or be embarrassing for everyone. Classes and programs and committees and missions efforts chug along with enviable consistency. In any church lobby, narthex, or fellowship hall on a Sunday morning you'll see hugs and handshakes and hear a buzz of conversation. People participate in their small groups / community groups / home groups / discipleship groups / missional communities / Sunday-school classes. It all just seems to work with no obvious upheaval.

But this is not unity. Under the surface in *any* church there is upheaval—of souls, of minds, of plans, in relationships, in church leadership, in local or global events. Unity is not found in ignoring or glossing over these difficult issues. The painted-on smiles and passive-aggressive responses (those responses where a harsh judgment is veiled in pleasantness, like "Bless your heart" or "Well, that apple fell far from the tree") prevalent in many churches do-not bind the people of God more closely together. Instead they communicate that it's not safe to talk about *those* issues here. Your upheaval must be dealt with privately or elsewhere, but not in church.

Niceness, stolidness, and pleasantness are all good and they all make it easy to walk in and settle into a community of believers. But what keeps us there through life's difficulties? When your marriage is on the rocks, will niceness get you the help you so desperately need? When the political climate is explosive, will pleasantness keep your church from fracturing? When there is simmering animosity between church members, will stolidness bring about reconciliation? No. Niceness and friendliness can actually lead to fractures in a church if people hide behind them from honesty and humility.

THE FAUX UNITY OF "AGAINSTNESS"

"The enemy of my enemy is my friend." This could easily be one of the core values of many churches. We have discovered that it's easy to build a congregation by finding a common enemy, something we are opposed to or want to distance ourselves from. We are unified in our opposition to this or that political party, this or that theological camp, this or that social movement. This mindset might be militant and outspoken, or it might be a more subtle set of cultural values. It often feels very tight-knit, and when you are part of it you feel very much the insider, very much like you're serving a cause, and therefore very much like you truly belong.

There are at least four significant problems with this mindset in the church.

First, being defined by what we are opposed to means that we are not setting a course but rather having our course dictated to us. We are constantly reacting, having our next step determined for us, rather than relentlessly moving forward on the mission of God.

Second, when we abide in this mindset we are constantly looking for enemies. We are predisposed to suspicion and rejection. Instead of the church being a hospital for the sick and a bright light in a dark place, it comes to resemble a little boy's treehouse with a "No gurlz allowed" banner and a double secret super password. It acknowledges Jesus' words to "love your enemies," but prefers to "love" them from a distance and with imprecatory prayers and aggressive evangelism.

Third, this perceived unity is shallow and short-lived.

It is shared fervor, but what happens when the threat dissipates or when culture shifts? We have to find a new issue or group to oppose. What happens if I change my mind or soften my views? All of a sudden I am on the outside, the recipient of judgment or pity.

Fourth, and most significantly, this is not at all the picture of Christian unity in the church that the Bible invites us into. True Christian unity is about the whole person and the whole body of believers, not about an issue or a group of people. It is positive unity centered on being for Christ (and him being for us), rather than a negative unity focused on being against something or someone. It is complex and expansive and inviting because it is a miracle brought about by the Holy Spirit through the work of the gospel in a body of believers.

THE BEAUTY AND BELONGING OF BIBLICAL UNITY

It is much easier to determine where we don't belong than where we do. We don't find belonging at churches that disguise disunity behind friendliness or that unify around causes and issues that aren't Jesus. We don't find belonging at churches that are openly contentious. And we don't find belonging at churches that make the gospel of Jesus Christ second to anything. It's not so easy to determine where we do belong. What does true unity in a church look like? As in all complex situations that require discernment, the Bible is the best place to turn.

The Mind of Christ

Every attempt at unity centers around something. We are unified in our love of a team, our dislike of a political candidate, our passion for a cause, our enjoyment of a hobby or activity, or even our affection for each other. And in every case, the unity is temporary and fragile because the thing binding people together is not strong enough to overcome differences, to bear the weight of change, or it simply fades away over time.

The church is called to be unified around Jesus Christ. He is the one in whom, through whom, by whom, and for whom we are bound together. And that bond in Jesus shapes and directs our affection, our causes, and our mission.

Philippians 2:2-5 says:

> *Complete my joy by being of the same mind, having the same love, being in full accord and of one mind. Do nothing from selfish ambition or conceit, but in humility count others more significant than yourselves. Let each of you look not only to his own interests, but also to the interests of others. Have this mind among yourselves, which is yours in Christ Jesus.*

Two particular phrases in these verses help describe true unity for us: "of the same mind" and "have this mind among yourselves, which is yours in Christ Jesus." If all we had was the first phrase it would be easy to think the Bible is saying, *be homogenous, agree on everything, and think just like everyone else.* That sounds more like cult-ish brainwashing than anything. But the second phrase expands our understanding: we are to have the mind found in Christ Jesus. That sounds much more promising, but what does it mean, exactly?

The middle of the passage shows that unity in Christ is reflecting Jesus to one another. When Paul says to "have this mind among yourselves," he's talking about the mind of the one who "did not count equality with God a thing to be grasped, but emptied himself, by taking the form of a servant" (Philippians 2:6-7). Christian unity starts with a transformation of our minds toward Christ-likeness, which will be evidenced especially in the attitude of humility and the action of serving one another.

So how do we get this mind of Christ? Many religions demand that their followers strive for a higher level of consciousness, or a certain amount of moral goodness, or gain a level of learning, in order that they can discover the true depths and wonders those religions offer. But 1 Corinthians 2:16 says simply, "We have the mind of Christ." If you are a follower of Jesus, a believer in his gospel, *you already have the mind of Christ.*

We do not gain some level of higher thought or consciousness through our own efforts. We already have the very Spirit of God who searches and knows the mind of God (1 Corinthians 2:10-12). This is the same Holy Spirit who Jesus promised to send to be our helper, our guide, and to declare to us the words of God.

If you are a Christian, you have the presence of Christ dwelling in you in the person of the Holy Spirit. If you are a Christian you are in Christ, wrapped up in his salvation and kingdom, joined to him for all eternity. So you have the mind of Christ, alongside every other Christian in the world. In Christ and his Spirit you and everyone else in your church have all you need to be a truly unified body and family of God.

A Christ-Shaped Life

One of the best (and occasionally most infuriating) things about how God speaks to us through his word is that he makes the applicability absolutely clear and inescapable. When the Bible lays out a truth as magnificent and expansive as the one we just saw, it always shows us how to live in that reality too. God does not want to blow our minds and then leave us lost. He invites us into the amazing freedom and joy of living as people who actually have the mind of Christ. One of the clearest such invitations is Ephesians 4:1-7.

> *I therefore, a prisoner for the Lord, urge you to walk in a manner worthy of the calling to which you have been called, with all humility and gentleness, with patience, bearing with one another in love, eager to maintain the unity of the Spirit in the bond of peace. There is one body and one Spirit—just as you were called to the one hope that belongs to your call— one Lord, one faith, one baptism, one God and Father of all, who is over all and through all and in all. But*

grace was given to each one of us according to the measure of Christ's gift.

Paul urges us, collectively, to "walk in a manner worthy of the calling to which we have been called." What calling is he referring to? In Ephesians 2 he laid out the miracle of new life through Christ and how in Christ there is no longer a dividing wall between people but rather oneness. So he is saying that being raised from death in sin to life in Jesus means we are one with everyone else who is in Christ, and this is our calling, our new way to live.

Humility, gentleness, patience, and bearing with one another in love are the marks of a Christ-shaped life and a Christ-shaped church. And they are not an end in themselves, but a means because we are also to be "eager to maintain the unity of the Spirit." So our walking according to our calling is done in pursuit of unity of the Spirit—unity in Christ. And because we often take our eyes off the mark, Paul makes sure we remember the foundations, the essentials: "one body and one Spirit ... one Lord, one faith, one baptism, one God and Father of all, who is over all and through all and in all."

What a magnificent, miraculous picture Paul is painting with these words! We are unified because of Christ and also in Christ. We share a single faith. We have one God who is our Father, so we are family. And he is the ruler and sustainer of all things. Verse 7 caps it off with an outpouring of hope and promise: "Grace was given to each one of us according to the measure of Christ's gift." We do not live out this calling in our ability and perseverance—we could not. Instead we receive the gift of grace, and not just a little. It is given "according to the measure of Christ's gift"—it is immeasurable and bottomless. God has called us to unity in Christ and promised us his grace without measure to obey what we are called to. He *really* wants his church to be one, and he really wants us to find belonging in it.

Unified in Love

Colossians 3:13-14 tells us we are to live in unity by "bearing with one another and, if one has a complaint against another, forgiving each other; as the Lord has forgiven you, so you also must forgive. And above all these put on love, which binds everything together in perfect harmony." It sounds strikingly like Ephesians 4, until that little phrase, "above all." When the writers of Scripture put that kind of emphasis on something, we should lock in. Paul is telling us what is the most important thing, the thing that holds all these other commands together: it is love.

We should wear love like a team uniform. All the other qualities we are called to in the previous verses flow out of love. What is humility or gentleness or forgiveness without love? Hollow, phony, incomplete. What is unity without love? Impossible, because only love binds everything, including us, together in perfect harmony.

Not only that, but love is the very thing that announces to the world that we are in Christ. John 13:35 tells us, "By this all people will know that you are my disciples, if you have love for one another." It is not primarily our doctrine, nor our mission or our causes, nor even our love for those outside the church, that shows we are Christ's. It is our *love for one another*—our true Christian unity.

LIVING IN UNITY

You and I need this. And we need to commit ourselves to it. Such unity did not come cheap. Jesus laid down his life so we could become his family and be one body in him. He called us to love one another so that the world would be compelled to notice and to want in on this magnificent reality, to find belonging among his people.

Unity does not come easy. Look around at the church; such beautiful unity is a rarity, a true miracle. But it is possible, in the power of the Holy Spirit by the grace of God. Don't think of it as something *I* devote myself to, but rather something that *Christ* is devoted to and that I am part of. He loves his Church, and yearns for you to be part of it—not just showing up, but really belonging, and offering that sense of belonging to the world in truth, love, safety, compassion, patience, and forgiveness.

To describe this magnificent reality is to paint a picture of peace, but unity among believers is not some Zen-like calm. Christian unity is not Christian utopia. Jesus said "Blessed are the peacemakers," (Matthew 5:9) because peace doesn't just happen, it must be made, fought for, defended, and clung to like our lives depend on it. Satan will do all he can to drive a wedge between us, so the peacemakers in the church are the ones who guard against those divisions and shore up all that unites us. First and foremost, this means valuing Jesus Christ and our brothers and sisters in Christ more than anything else.

When we encounter someone in the church who holds strongly to a different viewpoint or perspective on something significant like politics or church polity or even theology, what does unity look like? It begins by remembering that he is your brother in Christ. Christ did for him all that Christ did for you. It is safeguarded as we remember that the realities of the gospel are too wonderful to be sacrificed on the altar of opinion or preference or interpretation. So we view our brother in the best light, as a fellow child of God. We assume the best about him—that he is a person of godly character seeking to honor Jesus with his life too. When we start here, there is little room for animosity. Maybe the disagreements can be set aside altogether. After all, despite what social media would have us believe, we don't need to wage every war of words and win every argument. If, in good conscience, you feel you must address the disagreement then do so in person, charitably, with open ears—the way you would want someone to confront you. And do so outside of church gatherings, in a more private context, because, despite your differences, you are part of the same body worshiping the same God together. Disagreement doesn't need to be disunity and, in fact, can lead to greater trust and unity if handled with humility.

When someone in the church hurts you, the last thing you usually want is to be particularly unified to her. But she is your sister in Christ, and Christ is above all. So rather than ignoring the pain and pretending it doesn't exist or allowing bitterness to fester, seek to clean the wound. If you refuse to do this, you are multiplying the wrong done to you and threatening the unity of the church. Unaddressed wounds get infected. Infection spreads and begins to affect the rest of the body. Instead, approach her with honesty, humility, and honor, speaking the truth of your hurt without insult or accusation. In doing so, you are giving an opportunity for the Holy Spirit to work in her and to open her eyes (and to work in you and open yours, if that's necessary). When this happens, restoration and healing happen. The body is unified, and is left even stronger than it was.

This idea of fighting and working for unity might sound at odds with belonging. But it is more a statement of the beauty and immense value of unity in Christ. We fight for what we love, and we love each other as the family of God. We work and struggle to maintain and foster peace, for a place of belonging in Christ. And we do so side by side, growing in unity as we go.

ACTION STEPS

- If unity doesn't mean unanimity or sameness, what does it mean? Define it in biblical terms.

- It's easy to point out where other people are fractious or divisive, but consider in what ways *you* might be at risk of hindering that kind of unity. What might need to change in your heart and attitude so you *want* to be unified to those different than you or with whom you disagree?

- Unity doesn't come naturally, especially since churches are gatherings of disparate sinners. So we must work for it, invest in it, and defend it. Think about those with whom you find unity hardest. Here is an opportunity to fight for *gospel* unity. What would that look like for you?

- Reflect on the shared beliefs, loves, and passions of Jesus followers. They are so much deeper and richer and more defining than any opinion or position we hold about anything else. Keep these at the forefront of your mind and pray them into your heart. These are the unifiers of the church.

5. WHAT DO I
DO WHEN...

I fell in love with the *Calvin & Hobbes* comic strips and books when I was a kid and my enjoyment of them has not abated at all over the past 30-plus years. In one strip, Calvin is very excited about building a model airplane. He imagines the majestic fighter jet and is lost in rapture at the beauty of it. He pictures the sleek design and intimidating array of weapons and can't wait to see the final product. Of course, the actual building of the plane goes terribly awry (which is to be expected when a six-year-old tries to do detailed work or follow instructions), and what he ends up with is a sort of Frankenstein's-monster-meets-Picasso-painting contraption dripping with excess glue. Needless to say, Calvin is not pleased.

Often, our experience with church resembles this. We picture something beautiful, sleek, and powerful. We have visions of how wonderful it is going to be, how easily we will fit in, how perfect a fit it will be for us. But then we find instead something unpleasant, ineffective, or otherwise less than we hoped for. The reality of churches often falls far short of our visions, which leaves us with the difficult and complicated question of what it means to belong to a church that fails in some way. In this chapter I will seek to answer this question by looking at three different categories of frustration you may encounter at church: feeling like you don't belong, being disappointed by your church, and being hurt by your church. Most of us will experience the first two and, sadly, the third is fairly common as well, so feel free to jump to the category most pertinent to you.

WHAT DO I DO WHEN I DON'T FEEL I BELONG?

Throughout this book I have tried to build an understanding of belonging in church that is rooted in biblical definitions and perspectives. What it means to "belong" to a church is much more significant and substantial than a mere feeling of comfort or similarity, so this question applies to the definition and understanding I have sought to establish. It assumes that you see the church as a place God intends for you to belong and that you understand you are part of the family, part of the body, part of the structure. So you must evaluate the church, and yourself, according to that deeper, more substantial standard.

Ask, "Is There the Aroma of Christ in This Church?"

Over the years, I have attended and been a member of churches where I began to sense that maybe I did not belong there. It didn't feel right. Something was off. Maybe you have had a similar experience. My instinct was to run through a checklist of things every good church should have: biblical preaching, a strong doctrinal statement, meaningful and biblical music, opportunities for community, and so on. In most cases the churches checked each box (otherwise I wouldn't have joined them in the first place). Something else was amiss.

For many years I could not identify what it was. It was sort of the barometric pressure of church health—I could feel the ache a little bit and I knew it indicated something, but it was invisible to me. I've come to realize that it is the culture of the church, *the aroma of Christ* (2 Corinthians 2:15-16), that was missing. Did the people of the church, starting with the leaders, exude the welcome of Jesus? Was it marked by humility, by gentleness, by honesty and by honor? Did the preaching help us see and feel the love and forgiveness and very heart of Jesus, or did it burden us with law and guilt? Was it clear that the whole service centered on Jesus in worship and praise and reverence and joy? Sure the programs might be well run and the teaching content might be solid and trustworthy, but if a church does not exude the attitude and heart of Jesus then, yes, something is off.

In Revelation 2 we read the first of Jesus' seven letters to churches, addressed to the church in Ephesus. He commends them for their good works, their faithfulness to truth, and their endurance. But then Jesus says,

"You have abandoned the love you had at first" (2:4). This church checked the boxes of "a healthy church" in terms of their doctrine and effort, but they were, in truth, not healthy at all, for they lacked passion and life in Christ. Their good works and steadfastness to truth were missing something that Jesus deemed of utmost importance: a love for Jesus in response to his love for them. If you find yourself feeling like you don't belong, like your seemingly healthy church is missing something, it might be the love and aroma of Christ.

Self-evaluate and Audit
So when you feel that you don't belong at a church, it may be that your church is missing something vital. But it may also be that you are missing something, or missing an opportunity for something. Biblical belonging requires investment and commitment, as we've seen. So are you doing your part? Are you giving the church everything you can?

This will vary from person to person and situation to situation. We have people who come into our church exhausted, wounded, cynical, fearful, or simply just brand-new to the Christian faith. What they are able to give the church (and what the church ought to ask of them) is massively different from someone who comes in healthy, vibrant, energized, and mature in faith. For the first group, all they can give might be their presence, their listening ear, their willingness to take a risk by being honest, and their questions. The second group can give their whole selves to the church with joyful abandon and energy. You may be more like the first group or the second group, or somewhere in the middle, but having worked that out, if you want to belong to the church then give all you can.

The "one another" commands in Scripture that we looked at in chapter 3 (love one another, build one another up, bear with one another, forgive one another, serve one another, be devoted to one another, pray for one another, instruct one another, live in harmony with one another, submit to one another, honor one another, welcome one another, encourage one another, exhort one another) are two-way streets. You cannot truly belong to a body if you expect to receive these but are unwilling to give them, or you keep score and then scale back when you feel you're giving more than you're getting. When you feel like you don't belong in a church, it may be that you are holding back your heart in one or more of these commands and are creating distance where it need not exist.

One practical, but challenging, area to self-evaluate is that of time. Have you given your church enough time? Often our initial impressions are inaccurate, both of people and churches. We catch them on a down day or in an odd season. I spoke to a man recently who told me his initial impression of our church was that it was very focused on giving and money and he found this off-putting. Well, he had visited for the first time during a brief capital campaign when we were, in fact, talking a lot about giving and money. It took him time (thankfully he was patient) to realize there was much more to the church than that. In the same way that it takes time to get to know the true, good character of a person, it takes time to know the true, good culture and character of a church.

One final question to ask yourself is whether you are equating preferences with non-negotiables. It is easy to judge the "goodness" or "health" of a church by whether it fits our preferences. It is fine to have preferences about music, preaching style, small groups, Sunday-school classes, kids programs, or whatever. It is problematic when we make our preferences the righteous standard for a church. Your preferences do not supersede or define the aroma of Christ in a church. So preferences will inevitably influence your decision about joining a church, but don't let them move you toward judgment or disparagement, because that will keep you from finding belonging.

But how can we accurately and humbly weigh our preferences? Having preferences is inevitable; we all like some things more than others. But how do we make decisions based off these in church? When we're ordering food at a restaurant we simply choose what we like; it's the same when we decide what music to play in the car or what shoes to buy. But the church isn't a provider of goods and services and we aren't consumers, so we need a different value system for our preferences. In most cases it isn't black and white, right and wrong.

Here are a few questions to ask as you consider how to make decisions based off your preferences.

1. *Does your preference reflect a biblical priority or is it self-serving?*

    We occasionally have people leave our church to join a church closer to where they live—not because it is more convenient (though it is) but because they want to invest in biblical community where their life is centered. At the same time, we also have people who drive 40+ minutes to be part of our church because they feel called to love and serve here. We have people who leave because they desire a more (or less) liturgical service, and in both cases they are seeking a form of worship that allows them to express their heart before the Lord more fully. All these decisions could have been made for selfish reasons, but in each case that I am thinking of, the decision was made carefully, and prayerfully, and humbly. But it is key to challenge yourself about your own preferences.

2. *Is your preference an expression of fear, desire for control, or closed-mindedness?*

    It is so easy to attach moral value to matters of preference (just ask my kids how strongly I feel about the "right" way to load the dishwasher!). Often when we do this it reveals something in our hearts and lives that needs challenging: we are afraid of change, we want things our way, or we are simply unaware of new (and maybe better) ways of doing things.

So we plant a moral flag on a matter of preference and begin advocating for it and maybe even waging war over it. If we feel strongly that our preference is "right" but are unable to both articulate why from a biblical perspective and listen humbly to alternative perspectives, we likely have made an idol out of a preference.

3. *Can you set aside your preference for the sake of unity in the church?*

Unity cannot happen if we all die on the hills of our preferences. So we must ask ourselves if we are able to lay ours down and "count others more significant" than ourselves (Philippians 2:3). If the answer is no, we need to revisit the two questions above. Is it a biblical, God-honoring preference? Or is my heart clinging to an idol? If the answers to these questions are yes and no, respectively, then that preference becomes the basis for deciding whether to leave a church. If, however, you can set it aside then you are contributing further to the unity of that body.

What if the Church Doesn't Have the Aroma of Christ?

It is a difficult and often heartbreaking realization to see that your church lacks a Jesus-reflecting culture. What are you called to do then? Very simply, I would say *be* the culture you yearn to see. Be humble. Be honest. Be honoring. Be full of rejoicing. Jesus is magnetic and contagious. Others in the church are likely aching for the same thing, and when they see you modelling this attitude, it may inspire them to join in this real Christian community. Don't just hope that they will notice how you do things, though. Invite people into this culture with you. God uses vibrant, faithful Christians to breathe the life of Christ into stultified, stoic, cold churches.

Pursue and live out gospel culture in your church until you cannot. Pray for perseverance. Pray for spiritual fruit and life. Pray for strength and joy in the Lord. And yet a time may come when moving on is necessary. This isn't a sin or even a failure, even though you may well feel like it is. If you leave a church, leave well. Leave with the same humility, honesty, and honor you poured into it. (Honesty, in this case, might mean having a conversation with a pastor as to your reasons for moving on, being forthright without being accusatory.) Leave with gratitude for what God did do through your time as part of that church, not just sadness or frustration at your departure. You gave yourself to it for a time in hopes that God would do great things through that body, and when you leave remember it is still Christ's body, and continue yearning for the same works of God in and through it.

WHAT DO I DO WHEN THE CHURCH DISAPPOINTS ME?

Your church will disappoint you—no question. Every church you are ever part of or could ever be part of will disappoint you. The only way to avoid disappointment in a church is to expect nothing of it in the first place, in which case, why would you be part of a church at all?! Think of the imagery we looked at in chapter 2 that Scripture uses to describe the church: a family, a body, a building. Families have friction and conflict, even the relatively healthy ones. A healthy family is not one without conflict, but one that handles their inevitable conflicts well. However, some families are downright dysfunctional or full of animosity. (If your church is like this, the next section on being hurt by the church is likely for you, and you would be wise to seek a healthy church family).

Bodies get sick. Joints ache or blow out. Muscles pull and tear. Bones break. Allergy season lays a body low. Even healthy people get random headaches and scratchy throats.

Buildings crumble and decay. The plumbing leaks. The mortar crumbles. Storms rip the shingles off. Dust gathers in every corner. Constant maintenance is required just to keep a building from falling apart.

The church is a coalition of sinners, a collection of failures, and a gathering of the dysfunctional; including you and me. So of course we will disappoint one another. The question we face is what to do when that happens.

Our instinct is to think that something which disappoints us has failed us. A better instinct to develop would be to question our expectations. Every disappointment is an unmet expectation, so when the church disappoints us we need to be confident that our expectations are right and fair and biblical. You and I are part of that sinner/ failure/dysfunctional group, so it stands to reason that our expectations might not be perfect.

Ask yourself the following three questions, taking some time to really consider them.

1. *Can I specifically articulate my expectations for the church?*

   Frustrations and disappointments are easier to articulate than expectations or hopes, so it is often easier to complain about what you don't like than to explain what it is you hope for. One problem with this is that often your complaints don't touch on the heart of the issue. For example, you might say "I don't like how we run small groups," but your hope is "I want a few close friends in this church who I can be accountable to and who really build me up in my faith." It is helpful to be able to clearly state what you *expect* and *want* the church to do or be, because until you can articulate the expectation behind the disappointment you won't be able to resolve it.

2. *Are my expectations driven more by preferences or biblical values?*

   We touched on this earlier in the chapter. Once you have articulated your expectations you need to take them to the Bible and see what it has to say. Scripture will not always address particular preferences (music style, sermon length, program format, and so on). But it addresses the heart of the Christian, the shape of true worship, the centrality of the gospel, the foundational nature of the Bible, and so forth. Traditional hymns are not necessarily more or less biblical than more contemporary styles of music, but our willingness to worship with an open heart and our humility toward those who disagree is a deeply biblical issue. The Bible may not change our preferences but it will change our hearts—and that will change how much we cling to preferences.

3. *Are my expectations self-serving or selfless?*
   The biggest change in heart we usually need when it comes to preferences and disappointment is a move from selfish to selfless. We instinctively put ourselves first: "I like," "I prefer," "_____ would work best for me." That is an enemy of unity, and a hindrance to your belonging and the belonging of those around you. Being part of a church means being willing to hold preferences loosely for the good of the body and lay them down completely if that is best for the unity of the body. As we've seen, Philippians 2:3-4 urges us to "do nothing from selfish ambition or conceit, but in humility count others more significant than yourselves. Let each of you look not only to his own interests, but also to the interests of others." If we are disappointed and frustrated in a church, we need first to examine our own hearts. Are we willing to die to ourselves for the sake of the body, or would we rather die on the hill of our preferences?

You may well find yourself in a position where you can carefully, humbly articulate your expectations. They are biblical and you are, to the best of your ability, putting the needs and preferences of others first. You desire unity. Yet the church, be it your fellow members or the leadership, keeps letting you down in some manner—choosing to go in a direction that you disagree with, investing in aspects or areas of ministry you see as less important in the mission of the church, and so on. In this case it may be time to consider finding a new church home. I encourage you to revisit what I wrote on pages 90-91. Leaving a church because of perpetual disappointment and frustration is so exhausting and saddening, but in the end it is better than staying if staying means fighting and becoming embittered toward God's people.

WHAT DO I DO IF THE CHURCH HURTS ME?

Few situations are more painful than finding a home at a church, connecting with God's people, putting your trust in them and in the leadership, and really *belonging*—only to be hurt or betrayed by those same people or leaders. This is distinct from disappointment. Disappointment wishes things were different and struggles to be satisfied, and we can be disappointed when people have done nothing wrong but simply gone in a direction we didn't prefer. Being hurt by people in a church happens when we are the victim of wrongdoing of some kind. It is crucial that we discern the difference, especially because disappointment often feels like hurt. We live in a time when our feelings are easily confused for moral standards: if you make me feel badly then you have wronged me. This simply isn't how the Bible defines wrongdoing, though, and it's why it's important that we run our feelings of hurt/disappointment through the filter questions in the previous section. Disappointment is real, hurt is real, and wrongdoing is real. If we are part of a church body and committed to unity in Christ, we need to respond well in each situation.

While we are all likely aware of explosive, divisive situations of abuse and wrongdoing in churches, hurt in the church is not generally headline-grabbing. Usually it is the result of pride, selfishness, gossip, or some other quiet sin. Usually it isn't noticed by the whole congregation, let alone social media or journalists. And we all experience this type of hurt. Since the church is a body of sinners, we will sin against one another and cause hurt, and we will be the recipient of wrongdoing and hurt by fellow Christians.

Again, a distinction must be made between being hurt *in* the church and being hurt *by* the church. To be hurt *in* the church simply requires one person sinning against you, and when it happens we are called to pursue reconciliation in the Lord (Matthew 18:15, 21-22). This means bringing honesty to bear by going to them to address the hurt that was caused in the hope that they will receive your words humbly, apologize, repent (change their ways to walk in a manner reflective of Jesus), and take the necessary steps to make things right. Then you forgive and can be restored in your relationship. The aim is not accusation, escalation, recompense, someone "getting their due," or public shaming, but reconciliation between family members—that is, unity in Christ.

Being hurt *by* the church is a different, more grievous (and thankfully, more rare) situation. To be hurt by the church means that there has been a systemic and cultural breakdown in the church. It means that gospel culture is not pervading from the top down, and the leaders are either guilty by passivity or participation (Acts 20:28-31). This can lead to harshness, defensiveness, mockery, animosity, or even abuses of power and cover-ups of wrongdoing. In many cases this is a low-grade issue rather than the kind of crisis or controversy that becomes public. Members are quietly hurt, there doesn't seem to be a path to reconciliation and righting wrongs, and often they (you) quietly depart saying nothing and carrying wounds.

What can you do when you are hurt by a church to which you belong? Here are some practical principles.

Speak the Truth in Love, Even to Power
While Christ's desire for his church is that it be a body marked by humility and serving others, with leaders as the chief servants who set the pace for humility, often power dynamics are still at play. Church leaders are authority figures, called to lead the congregation.

So confronting them on wrongdoing or even simply pointing out how they hurt you can be intimidating. It is difficult to look a spiritual authority figure in the face and say, "When you did X it hurt me." It can be terrifying to stand before a group of leaders and say, "I believe the way you are leading this church is unbiblical."

But our commitment to honesty before Christ compels us to do so when the need arises. And our commitment to honoring one another informs how we do it. Ephesians 4:15 tells us to speak the truth in love—the truth as defined by God's word and love as defined by the heart of Christ. This means speaking clearly and boldly about the wrongs done, and doing so in humility, respecting those to whom you speak, and with a deep desire for their best.

The heart behind a confrontation like this yearns for repentance and reconciliation. You want to see individual and corporate restoration, and faithfulness to Jesus, and this requires humility and openness on both sides. We are all sinners, so be willing to acknowledge the possibility of your own ignorance of a situation or that you may have contributed to the hurt. Sometimes, though, people stand firm in their sins, and confronting them may cost you—reputation, relationships, a church home. But standing firm in the truths of the Bible and lovingly presenting them to those who are in the wrong is always right, and God smiles on you for it.

Don't Give Up on the Church Because You've Been Hurt by a Church

If you have faithfully, lovingly confronted the wrongdoing of a church and its leaders, and if repentance and reconciliation are not the response, then it will likely be necessary to leave that church. Leaving a church you love is always difficult. Leaving a church you loved and that seemingly turned on you is brutal. And the last place you'll likely be inclined to turn is to another church. Entrusting yourself to another group of leaders and another congregation could easily feel like an impossible risk because of the pain and the anger at the betrayal.

Yet the church is the only place we can heal from the hurt we've encountered in church. It sounds counterintuitive, and that's because it is. In a fallen world we can easily be hurt in the church, but the answer is not to abandon it, because in that fallen world we desperately need the body of Christ. We need a local body, a gathering body, not just a generalized global aggregate of Christians. Nowhere else in the world will you ever encounter the wound-healing, grace-giving, come-as-you-are, we're-with-you, day-by-day love of Jesus. So take the risk, but feel free to take it slowly. Seek out other churches. Sniff the air for the aroma of Christ. Test the waters for honesty and honor and safety. Don't feel the need to rush, but don't drift away either. One church's failure is not the failure of Christ's gospel or his plan, nor does it reflect Christ's heart for you. He has a place for you among his people where you can belong.

ACTION STEPS

- Pray for humility and discernment. So often our perception of the church and how we feel about it is flavored by our own pride, our past experiences, or our misperceptions of what is going on. We all need the Holy Spirit's help.

- Eschew gossip and complaining. When we feel dissatisfied at a church or as if we don't belong it is so easy to complain to others. But negativity and mistrust spreads like mold. Rather than sharing complaints, seek out those with the capacity to influence change and speak openly and humbly with them. Pray with trusted friends. But don't spread the rot of gossip and complaint.

- Forgive others as God has forgiven you in Christ. When you are hurt in church, pursue forgiveness. This doesn't necessarily mean you shouldn't move on or that you can instigate reconciliation; that takes both parties after all. But don't let bitterness take root in your heart. It will poison your soul, and, in time, those around you.

6. JESUS, FRIEND
OF SINNERS

I have two teenage daughters who are both bright, strong-willed young women. It would be fair to call these genetic traits, and so when we argue it can be quite a battle. Given that I am the authority figure (for now), I am more educated (for now), I am wiser (for now), and I am older I usually come out the winner of these battles, much to their chagrin. More than once I have heard one of them mutter, "Why do you have to be so *smart*?" or "Ugh, you *always* have the answers to *everything*" as they skulk away. They mean this as an insult, but it's actually pretty high, if not always accurate, praise.

When people called Jesus a "friend of tax collectors and sinners" (Matthew 11:19; Luke 7:34) it was a bit like this, only much weightier and more truthful. They intended to insult him and accuse him but were unknowingly honoring him for a beautiful aspect of his identity and nature. They were intending to number Jesus among the unworthy, the filthy, the shameful. Instead they were accidentally declaring the hope of salvation for the unworthy, the filthy, and the shameful. The accusation didn't bring Jesus low, it revealed his heart for sinners—a heart that you and I desperately need because without it we would have no hope of belonging.

HOW JESUS DEFINES "FRIEND"

Jesus doesn't want us in any doubt how he sees himself: he is our friend. He makes this clear in John 15:13-17 and he lays out, in precise terms, what it means that he is our friend and we are his.

> *Greater love has no one than this, that someone lay down his life for his friends. You are my friends if you do what I command you. No longer do I call you servants, for the servant does not know what his master is doing; but I have called you friends, for all that I have heard from my Father I have made known to you. You did not choose me, but I chose you and appointed you that you should go and bear fruit and that your fruit should abide, so that whatever you ask the Father in my name, he may give it to you. These things I command you, so that you will love one another.*

He declares that the truest, most loving friend is the one who lays down his life for his friends, which is really a declaration of his own great love and friendship. But pause and think about this for a moment. For whom did Jesus die? Sinners, the unworthy, the spiritually dead, yes—but here he says that he laid down his life *for his friends*. So Jesus declared himself a friend—the best and most loving friend—of sinners like you and me.

Jesus then says that we are his friends if we keep his commands. At first this looks like pettiness, an elementary-school-level tactic: Jesus' version of, "Give me half your lunch every day and we can be friends." But Jesus isn't setting up a bar we must clear or an entry fee to friendship. He is defining the nature of his commands. They aren't burdensome laws meant to crush or complicated hoops through which we must jump. They are invitations to walk with him, to stay close to him, to find the way of true and eternal life through him. Friendship with Jesus is not friendship with a peer. It is not equal give-and-take. We have *nothing* to offer Jesus. He is the Creator, the King, the Lord of the universe. For him to befriend us is nothing but mercy and kindness, and his commands are those of a merciful King and Holy God. So keeping the commands of Christ is the clearest outward evidence of our friendship with him.

He calls us friends, not servants. The Son and heir gave us the message and the call and the promise that the Father gave him. So we are not blindly obeying commands and serving out of obligation. We are participating in the life of the household of God as children and friends. We are participants in a grand, eternal plan with a certainty of arriving in glory.

Finally, Jesus called us and befriended us *so that* we would love one another. The friendship of Jesus is not merely something we accept and benefit from. It is transformative, turning us into Christ-reflecting friends for one another. Jesus' commands aren't given just so that we will stay close to him, but to form us so that we can love others the way he loved us. And how did Jesus love us? By laying down his life for his friends. Jesus ends where he began, by defining love and friendship by total self-sacrifice and calling all his followers and friends to follow him into it.

HOW JESUS SHOWS HIS FRIENDSHIP

When you think of the close friends you've had, those who have left the most positive imprint on your life, what are some of the defining characteristics of those people and relationships? I would venture to guess that the list includes several of the following:

- They are trustworthy and reliable; you can count on them.

- They are honest and open, keeping no secrets and sharing what's really going on in their hearts and lives.

- They listen well and absorb what you share with understanding.

- They are fun and you share common interests and a wealth of stories about experiences you've had.

- They have overcome challenges and walked

through adversity or suffering with you and you with them.

- They are willing to sacrifice for you and are generous with their resources.

- You've developed familiarity and closeness so they know how you are and when things aren't right.

- They are willing to say the hard things to you when you need it, for your good.

- They want the best for you; they celebrate with you when it happens, and grieve with you when it doesn't.

These are Christ-reflecting characteristics. They are good and beautiful. Yet they pale in comparison to the magnificent ways that Jesus showed his friendship to sinners like us. You may never have really considered Jesus as your friend, or on the other hand maybe the following verses and statements will be familiar to you, but don't let familiarity breed boredom. As you read, take a moment to reflect and marvel at each of the ways Jesus shows himself to be your friend.

He set aside his own glory to become one of us (Philippians 2:6-8). Jesus was enthroned in heaven as the Son of God, the Lord of the universe. He had no needs and lacked for nothing. Yet he "emptied himself, by taking the form of a servant, being born in the likeness of men. And being found in human form, he humbled himself" (Philippians 2:7). He carried out the mission of salvation that could only be completed by his willingness to lower himself. Why would he do this? Because he loves us. He came that we "may have life and have it abundantly" (John 10:10) and to make this happen he needed to step out of glory into humanity. And he did so without hesitation or regret.

He laid down his life for us (John 15:13). What more can a friend give than his life? You and I might think about the heroism required to die to save a friend or loved one. We might hope that if that moment ever arrived we would have the courage to do what was necessary. But that isn't exactly what Jesus did. Romans 5:7-8 tells us, "For one will scarcely die for a righteous person—though perhaps for a good person one would dare even to die—but God shows his love for us in that while we were still sinners, Christ died for us." He didn't die for those who were close to him. He died *so that* we could be close to him. He laid down his life to make us friends, not because we deserved it as friends.

He gave us his Spirit (John 16:7, 13-14). One of the most surprising sentences in the Bible is when Jesus says, "Nevertheless, I tell you the truth: it is to your advantage that I go away." He is saying that his followers would be better off if he left and returned to his Father's side. That doesn't sound at all like good friendship: "Look, it's better if I'm not around." But we need to let Jesus finish: "For if I do not go away, the Helper will not come to you.

But if I go, I will send him to you." He wasn't promising to leave us without his presence. He was promising that by his leaving, his presence—through the Holy Spirit—would be sent to be with *every believer*. It was to our advantage that Jesus left Earth because instead of Jesus being in one place at a time, connecting with a few followers, his Spirit now dwells in every follower of his, across the globe, for all time. He promised constant, faithful presence and friendship, and in giving us his Spirit, he kept that promise.

He brought us near to him and to one another (Ephesians 2:13-14). Ephesians 2:12 calls us, before we believed, "separated from Christ... having no hope and without God in the world." Basically, we had no business being friends of Jesus. We were alienated, opposed, antagonistic, apathetic, and rebellious. And, in sin, that is our posture toward other people as often as not, so we don't have any business being united or close to one another either. But God had different plans for us and worked them for us through his Son. "But now in Christ Jesus you who once were far off have been brought near by the blood of Christ. For he himself is our peace, who has made us both one and has broken down in his flesh the dividing wall of hostility." We have been brought near, out of alienation and separation. We have been brought near, overcoming our rebellion and apathy and antagonism. We have been brought near for unity with Christ, and through him with one another. Christ rescued us to make us friends with him and with each other.

He intercedes for us (Romans 8:34). A good friend stands up for his friends. He might take a beating for a friend or be punished for something he didn't do to cover for a friend. All that barely hints at what Romans 8:34 means when it says, "Christ Jesus is the one who died—more than that, who was raised—who is at the right hand of God, who indeed is interceding for us." He is not our peer, taking a bad rap for us. He is not our lawyer, representing us before God the Judge. He is not putting in a good word for us. He intercedes because he has done all that is necessary for us to be right with God by dying an innocent death and rising again from the dead and ascending to his Father's side in glory. So his intercession doesn't carry a tone of "Come on, Dad, give the poor guy a break." He isn't pleading our case. There's no need. Christ's intercession for us is a declaration that we are his, we are with him, we are cleansed by his blood, and we are wrapped in his righteousness.

He shared his inheritance with us (Romans 8:17). Jesus is the only begotten Son of God. He is the heir of all God's glory, and God has put everything under his rule and authority. And Romans 8:17 calls us "fellow heirs with Christ" because, as we saw in chapter 2, we are adopted as children of God. Christ shares his riches with us—riches of grace, forgiveness, restoration, and glory. He has lifted us out of squalor and we will reign with him forever. Jesus pours out blessings on friends for eternity.

When we call Jesus "friend of sinners," this is what we mean. He befriends us expecting nothing in return except faith, and he gives us everything he has despite us deserving nothing. His friendship is salvation itself.

A HOME FOR SINNERS

What does all this have to do with belonging to a church? Everything. The purpose of the church is to proclaim and exhibit the reality of Jesus Christ to the world. It is where and how people encounter the real Jesus. The old hymn, "Jesus, What a Friend for Sinners," describes him as "saving, helping, keeping, loving," and there could scarcely be a better description of the one who welcomes sinners and transforms them into members of God's family.

As a Christian, you have experienced this transformation and welcome from Jesus, so now you have the joy and privilege of extending it to others. We start doing this within our churches because "by this all people will know that you are my disciples, if you have love for one another" (John 13:35). Our love and friendship of fellow sinners within the church is Christ's witness to the world. It is a magnetic (and bizarre, given the world's expectations) invitation.

And we extend the welcome and friendship of Jesus to those who have yet to encounter it, all who feel themselves unworthy of it—the dirty, the ashamed, the drifting, the deconstructing, the outcasts. We have *been* these people, maybe very recently, so we know their need and we know the freedom and life found in the embrace of Jesus.

"Friend of sinners" is the very foundation of belonging in a church. Without it, none of us could belong. Jesus' friendship guarantees safety for the hurting and ashamed. It opens the door for real honesty. It is the model and empowerment for Christian unity. Friendship with Jesus fulfills our longings and shapes our future and direction. It defines our very purpose in life, to deeply enjoy the friendship of Jesus and display his loving heart to those around us. And the body of Christ, his church, is to be the context and environment and means of belonging for every Christian because it is where we exhibit and proclaim his friendship for sinners together.

This, then, is how to belong: follow in Jesus' footsteps, with the help of his Holy Spirit, by laying down your life for the benefit of your church and giving yourself joyfully and wholeheartedly to loving Jesus and his people. It is as you do this, and allow others to do this for you, that you will belong—and it is as you belong in this way that you'll enjoy the sweet, deep, refreshing fellowship for which you were created.

ACTION STEPS

- Do you wonder at, and are you inspired to worship by, how much Jesus has done for you in spite of how little you deserve? That realization and response is vital to a vibrant Christian life, and sharing it with others is what brings us together as the body of Christ. How can you make sure that wonder and praise are part of your daily life?

- The purpose of the church is to proclaim and exhibit the reality of Jesus Christ to the world, and we do this by being the same kind of friend to sinners that he was. How can you reflect the heart of Jesus to the people in your life so that they feel utterly loved and welcomed in church?

- How has this book changed your view of what gospel-belonging looks like in a local church? How are you being called to think differently? Love differently? Act differently?

DISCUSSION GUIDE FOR SMALL GROUPS

1. WHAT DOES IT MEAN TO BELONG?

1. What groups, communities, or causes do you belong to? What is good about each of them?

2. What makes the church similar to and different from those groups?

3. *Read Hebrews 10:23-25.* What are we called to do here, and what should the result be? How do we see both the moral obligation to belong and the goodness of belonging in these verses?

4. *Read John 17:20-26.* What does Jesus say he has already done and will do for us (v 22, 26)? What does he pray for us (v 21, 23-24)?

5. We'll look in more detail in future chapters at what it means to belong to the church. But for now, what do you think the "oneness" that Jesus talks about looks like (or could look like) in local churches today?

6. What will you pray for your church as a result of what you've read and discussed?

2. YOU BELONG

1. *Read Romans 8:14-17.* What difference does it make, according to this passage, to have been adopted into God's family? What impact might this have on our sense of belonging in church?

2. *Read 1 Corinthians 12:14-27.* What two key mistakes does Paul address in verses 14-20 and 21-26? What might it look like to make those mistakes, and how can we avoid them? (Read p 37-40 for more help with this.)

3. *Read Ephesians 2:19-22.* How do you respond to the idea that you are part of a "building"? How do you respond to the idea that you are part of God's "dwelling place" and "holy temple"?

4. Why is it tempting to think of God's mission as something pursued by "lone rangers"? Why is the kind of approach we read about in Acts 4:32-35 better? (See p 44-45.)

5. What are the implications of all these passages for the way we treat those who are suffering, those with particular gifts, and those who are part of the visible church community without being believers in Christ?

6. What is one step you could take to treat your fellow church members as family members or as fellow body parts? What difference will it make to remember that you are being built together into a temple and that God has designed you as his mission team to bring light into the world?

3. WHAT DOES IT LOOK LIKE TO BELONG?

1. *Read Matthew 9:10-13.* How can we learn from Jesus' words here in our churches today? What does it look like, practically, to show mercy to one another?

2. "The church is where God intends for Jesus to do his work [of cleansing and healing]" (p 56). Does this surprise you? How does James 5:16 say we gain healing?

3. Read p 57-59. Imagine you were getting ready to share something deep and honest with other church members. What difference would it make to you to meet with each of the three attitudes Piper describes?

4. *Read Ephesians 4:1-3.* What is freeing and/or what is intimidating about this calling for you personally?

5. Look at the list of "one anothers" on p 63-64. Which of these would you most like to get better at?

6. What step could you take together to build (even more of) a gospel culture in your church?

4. UNITY: THE ONLY WAY BELONGING HAPPENS

1. *Read Philippians 2:2-7.* How is each of Paul's commands in verses 2-5 exemplified by Jesus? How might they be exemplified by us?

2. *Read Ephesians 4:1-7.* Why should the statements in verses 4-7 lead to the actions described in verses 1-3?

3. Think of some disagreements or conflicts that might arise in a church. How does Ephesians 4:1-7 help us to discern which differences need to simply be laid aside and which should be pursued or dealt with? What impact does this passage have on how we go about resolving conflicts, disagreements, or hurts?

4. Piper writes that we already have the mind of Christ (p 74) and that God's grace equips us to obey (p 77-78). He also writes that we need to fight for unity (p 79-81). How does being aware of what we have been given in Christ motivate and help us to fight for unity?

5. *Read Colossians 3:12-14.* Discuss what unity through love looks like and how this is different from the unity of "niceness" or "againstness."

6. In what ways might your church be in danger of veering toward the unity of niceness or the unity of againstness? Be specific—what situations might lead to one or the other, and what are some ways to avoid basing your church unity on those two false unities?

5. WHAT DO I DO WHEN...

1. What kinds of things might (rightly or wrongly) make someone feel that they don't belong in church?

2. What are some good reasons to leave a church? What are some bad reasons?

3. *Read Revelation 2:1-7.* What was the problem with the church in Ephesus? What do you think this could look like in a church today?

4. What were the two possibilities for the future of the church in Ephesus? How might this encourage someone who is frustrated by the lack of love in their church?

5. What's the difference between being disappointed by church and being hurt by church (see p 95-97)? What's the difference in how we should respond?

6. Is there anything that might make it difficult for someone to feel that they belong in your church? What could you do to lay down your preferences for their sake?

6. JESUS, FRIEND OF SINNERS

1. *Read John 15:13-17.* What does it mean to be friends with Jesus, according to this passage?

2. Why is loving one another an essential result of being friends with Jesus?

3. Read through the statements in italics on p 105-108. Which of them do you find most striking or wonderful?

4. How could each of these truths about Jesus help us to gain a sense of belonging in the church?

5. How can you better reflect Jesus' character as a friend of sinners in your church? Come up with some specific ideas.

6. What is one thing you will change about your attitude or behavior toward others in your church as a result of reading this book?

RESOURCES FOR
SMALL GROUPS

Access the free small-group kit at loveyourchurchseries.
com. The free kit includes a video introduction to each
session as well as downloadable PDFs of a discussion
guide and worksheets. Each session is based on a chapter
of the book.

loveyourchurchseries.com

LOVE YOUR CHURCH

the**good**book
COMPANY

BIBLICAL | RELEVANT | ACCESSIBLE

At The Good Book Company, we are dedicated to helping Christians and local churches grow. We believe that God's growth process always starts with hearing clearly what he has said to us through his timeless word—the Bible.

Ever since we opened our doors in 1991, we have been striving to produce Bible-based resources that bring glory to God. We have grown to become an international provider of user-friendly resources to the Christian community, with believers of all backgrounds and denominations using our books, Bible studies, devotionals, evangelistic resources, and DVD-based courses.

We want to equip ordinary Christians to live for Christ day by day, and churches to grow in their knowledge of God, their love for one another, and the effectiveness of their outreach.

Call us for a discussion of your needs or visit one of our local websites for more information on the resources and services we provide.

Your friends at The Good Book Company

thegoodbook.com | thegoodbook.co.uk
thegoodbook.com.au | thegoodbook.co.nz
thegoodbook.co.in